# Summary Bundle: History & Finance | Readtrepreneur Publishing: Includes Summary of Red Notice & Summary of Rich Dad Poor Dad

# By: Bill Browder

**Proudly Brought to you by:**

## Legal Disclaimer

The information contained in this book is not designed to replace any professional medical advice. The information in this book has been provided for educational and entertainment purposes only.

The information contained in this book has been compiled from sources deemed reliable, and it is accurate to the best of the Author's knowledge; however, the Author cannot guarantee its accuracy and validity and cannot be held liable for any errors or omissions. Changes are periodically made to this book. You must consult your doctor or get professional medical advice before using any of the suggested remedies, techniques, or information in this book. Images used in this book are not the same as of those of the actual book. This is a totally separate and different entity from that of the original book titled: Red Notice

Upon using the information contained in this book, you agree that the Author is not liable for any damages, costs, and expenses, including any legal fees potentially resulting from the application of any of the information provided by this guide. This disclaimer applies to any damages or injury caused by the direct or indirect use and application of any advice or information, whether in breach of contract, tort, negligence, personal injury, criminal intent, or any other course of action.

You agree to accept all risks in using the information presented in this book. You need to consult a professional medical practitioner in order to ensure you are both able and healthy enough to participate in this program.

# Table of Contents

# The Book at a Glance

The author, Bill Browder, immediately strikes a chord of peril and suspense when he describes a "red notice" at the beginning of his book. A red notice is an international "be on the lookout" (or BOLO) announcement that informs the governments of practically every country that the International Police (or Interpol) requests the arrest of a particular person for a crime committed in at least one national jurisdiction.

In *Red Notice,* Browder tells a gripping story of how he got on the Interpol radar. It is a tale that intertwines the world of high finance with international politics, corruption, suspense, and betrayal.

That it is a non-fictional account makes the book all the more compelling.

Chapters 1 through 7 chronicle the origins of Browder's ancestors, as well as Browder's youth to his tentative first steps as an investment banker — a compelling tale in itself. Browder is the progeny of remarkably brilliant immigrants from Western Europe.

Chapter 8 onward is an enthralling voyage through the compelling quagmire that is the Russian economy right after the dissolution of the communist Soviet Union in the early 1990s, and its tentative and chaotic ascent (some say descent) into the capitalist world.

Russia is a country where you *"Ask a question, and get a riddle."* Many times, in Browder's own account, you ask a question, and you just end up with more questions. His fascination with his ancestors' homeland leads to his relocation to Eastern Europe and his first job in Russia.

He comes into his own as an investment banker as the communist experiment in Eastern Europe is unraveling. The atmosphere for entrepreneurship and adventure feels like a modern Gold Rush. Only this time, instead of unearthing gold nuggets, finance professionals salivate at the prospects of mining the economic assets of Eastern Europe and Russia, which are grossly undervalued (at least on paper).

His "shareholder activism" approach to investing puts him at odds with the Russian oligarchs divvying up the spoils of the Russian economy after the dissolution of the Soviet Union. It is estimated that the Russian oligarchs, most of whom operate with the (arguably corrupt) support of the Russian government, "stole" 40% of the country's assets mostly consisting of natural resources such as oil and gas. These oligarchs comprised a small cadre of about twenty men who became billionaires practically overnight.

As he tries to publicize the excesses of opportunistic oligarchs and a corrupt government under Putin, Browder is turned into Russia's Public Enemy Number One. At one point, he was CEO of the biggest foreign investor in Russia, but with the stroke of a pen, Browder's Russian visa is revoked after authorities label him as a threat to national security. He is expelled from the country, has his company assets seized, and sees his friends and associates systematically harassed, imprisoned, or even killed.

After his lawyer, Sergei Magnitsky, dies in prison under mysterious circumstances, Browder's role changes from being a high finance maverick to a human rights activist. He doggedly pursues the perpetrators who stole his company assets and caused Magnitsky's death.

In *Red Notice*, he attributes the revocation of his visa to his exposure of corruption at the highest levels of the Russian government. He is eventually convicted, tried, and sentenced *in absentia* by the Russian government for tax fraud (of which Magnitsky was also charged). Interpol, however, subsequently rejects any requests by the Russian government to arrest him, because the requests are based not on criminal activity but on politics.

His crusade for human rights is rewarded when both the United States and the European Community pass laws that impose diplomatic sanctions on countries guilty of human rights abuses against political prisoners. He continues his crusade to this day, and Russia still considers him an enemy.

Bill Browder is a Stanford-educated British citizen who was born in the United States in 1964. He gave up his American citizenship over 20 years ago to avoid taxes on his foreign investments earnings. He becomes the CEO of Hermitage Capital Management, an investment fund that he founded with Jewish billionaire Edmond Safra, who mysteriously dies in a fire in 1999 — an event that only adds to the drama surrounding Browder.

Browder lives in the United Kingdom and marries Sabrina Browder, with whom he has a son, Joshua Browder, who is himself an entrepreneur. He later marries a Russian, Elena Molokova, with whom he has two daughters. He starts his own website, *http://www.billbrowder.com* to chronicle his Russian (mis)adventures.

# FREE BONUSES

### P.S. Is it okay if we overdeliver?

Here at Readtrepreneur Publishing, we believe in overdelivering way beyond our reader's expectations. Is it okay if we overdeliver?

Here's the deal, we're going to give you an extremely condensed PDF summary of the book which you've just read and much more...

What's the catch? We need to trust you... You see, we want to overdeliver and in order for us to do that, we've to trust our reader to keep this bonus a secret to themselves? Why? Because we don't want people to be getting our exclusive PDF summaries even without buying our books itself. Unethical, right?

Ok. Are you ready?

Firstly, remember that your book is code: "**READ71**".

Next, visit this link: **http://bit.ly/exclusivepdfs**

Everything else will be self explanatory after you've visited: **http://bit.ly/exclusivepdfs**.

We hope you'll enjoy our free bonuses as much as we enjoyed preparing it for you!

# Chapter 1. Persona Non Grata

In November 2005, Bill Browder is returning to Russia. For some reason, he feels nervous as his plane approaches a country into which his investment firm had invested over $4.5 billion over the past ten years. After landing in Russia that evening, he is surprised by Russian officials, who take him into custody for unknown reasons and place him inside a detention room with some passengers.

He calls Elena, his girlfriend in the U.K., who at the time is carrying his child. He also calls Ariel, his Russian-based Jewish security consultant, and his contacts in the British embassy, neither of whom can ascertain the reason for his detention.

He is afraid because of his company, Hermitage Capital, has been attracting intense scrutiny from Russian officials. Browder ends up spending the night in the detention cell and is deprived of food and water. Frustrated and in rage, he bangs on the windows of the detention room to no avail.

The next morning, he is roughly and wordlessly taken from the detention area by Russian officials, who put him on the next flight back to London. He is thankful that he was not thrown into one of Russia's notorious prisons.

He arrives in London with no further incident and immediately ponders how he would return to his business in Russia — it is no longer a question of *when*, but *if*.

# Chapter 2. How Do You Rebel Against a Family of Communists?

Browder's fascination with Russia started with his Russian-born grandparents and great-grandparents. His Jewish grandfather, an ardent communist who ran for U.S. President, headed the U.S. Communist Party and even went to prison for his Communist sympathies. Earl Browder's involvement with the Communist party would affect his descendants' lives in ways he couldn't have imagined.

His father, Felix Browder, was a highly intelligent mathematician who enlisted in the U.S. Army before he was yanked from regular service and made to pump gas for army vehicles when officers found out he was Earl Browder's son. Only through Eleanor Roosevelt's intervention was Felix able to secure a teaching position at Brandies University.

On the other hand, Browder's mother, Eva Applebaum, had been put up for adoption as Eva's mother was trying to escape the clutches of Nazi Germany. Fortunately, Eva would make her way to the U.S. and become a brilliant academician herself, graduating from MIT. Browder's brother would graduate high school at 15 and become a Ph.D. student at 19; he is now one of the world's foremost particle physicists.

With this intellectual provenance, Bill Browder himself would become quite the brilliant student and achiever. At 13 years old, he is the youngest student at a Colorado boarding school, having skipped the eighth grade. He is bullied by the older students but fights back. He is eventually expelled from the boarding school and figures that (unlike his family) he is not cut out for the academic world. He wants to become a capitalist.

# Chapter 3. Chip and Winthrop

Being expelled from school, it is difficult for Browder to apply to top-tier schools. However, he somehow gets accepted to the University of Colorado in Boulder. During his sophomore year, he decides to go to a better school, gets straight A's, and transfers to the University of Chicago as an economics major.

With the fervor of capitalism raging inside him, he is advised that one of the best ways to jump into capitalist America is to become a scholar at a top consulting and financial company. He secures a scholarship from the illustrious consulting group Bain & Company, which helps him get into the acclaimed MBA program at Stanford University.

Before graduating from Stanford, Browder has a job interview with J.P. Morgan and is interviewed by two managers — Jake Chip Brant III and Winthrop Higgins IV ("Chip and Winthrop"). He is rejected, feels that he would not have fit into the stuck-up culture of the company with his grandparents' gritty, activist, American steelworker, union-type, blue-collar work ethic in his bones.

Instead, he gets a job at another esteemed consultancy firm, The Boston Consulting Group, where he immediately decides to return to his grandparents' ancestral homeland. He informs his puzzled new employers that he wants to work in Eastern Europe, and they quickly try to find a niche for their prized employee.

# Chapter 4. "We Can Get You a Woman to Keep You Warm at Night"

It is 1990, and the 26-year-old Browder's first boss in BCG, John Lindquist, is able to secure a position for Browder in the Eastern European branch of BCG in London, where he works for a terror named Wolfgang Schmidt. His first project is to restructure a Polish bus company.

Schmidt commands Browder to go to Sanok, Poland, to deal with the bus company employees. Browder immediately immerses himself in his work and realizes that the implosion of the Communist stranglehold in Eastern Europe and Russia has freed up previously state-owned companies for grabs by private investors — in a word, privatization.

In Sanok, the lure of the newly freed Eastern Europe feels like a drunken reverie on most nights. People are drinking and partying endlessly and Browder is told that "We can get you a woman to keep you warm at night."

However, Browder is getting drunk on something else: capitalism. He sees the immense profits that are at play. For example, the Polish bus company Autosan is valued for sale by the Polish government at $80 million despite having profits twice that amount the previous year. He successfully engineers the purchase of the company for BCG's client at a huge profit, but at an inadvertently horrendous cost — thousands of people are laid off to 'trim the fat' from the newly acquired company.

Saddened by the turn of events, he aspires to be an investor in similarly successful deals while avoiding the human cost of layoffs.

# Chapter 5. The Bouncing Czech

After his eye-opening Poland experience, Browder is assigned to write for the magazine, *Mergers and Acquisitions Europe*.

As part of his assignment, he decides to interview the enigmatic British-Czechoslovakian billionaire, John Maxwell. The representative that Browder is interviewing from John Maxwell's firm takes note of Browder's own Eastern Europe mergers and acquisitions experience and offers Browder a job in Maxwell's company with a higher salary. Browder accepts.

He begins working for the eccentric billionaire (who goes to work by helicopter); in Browder's first year, he is involved in three projects after reviewing over three hundred of them.

But disaster suddenly strikes. John Maxwell's operations, it turns out, has been bleeding cash, and the distraught billionaire commits suicide just as Browder sinks his teeth into investment banking. Unfortunately, Maxwell was the only major investment company investing in Eastern Europe.

John Maxwell's firm would eventually be liquidated, and Browder would soon be out of a job.

# Chapter 6. The Murmansk Trawler Fleet

The John Maxwell association leaves an indelible stain on Browder's resume. He gets interviews at some investment banks and joins the Salomon Brothers' investment banking unit, the only company seemingly willing to take a chance on him.

With Salomon Brothers, Browder gets his first experience in Russia. He is dispatched to Russia to assess the value and salability of the Murmansk Trawler Fleet, a large fishing operation.

While Murmansk only yields a small profit for Salomon, the greatest value of the experience is the revelation that Russia is an untapped goldmine. The Murmansk fleet is worth billions of dollars, yet the face value of investments under its name is only in the hundreds of millions.

Browder expects that his discovery would create a big buzz at Salomon. On the contrary, everyone ignores him until Bill Ludwig, a senior Salomon partner, gives him $25 million to start an investment program in Russia.

# Chapter 7. La Leopolda

Though Browder is now buying and trading securities and investing them in companies, ethics legislations based on the Chinese Wall mean that he can only work in one of the two capacities. Unable to secure an office in London, he sets up an office in Moscow.

He stumbles upon the voucher system in the Russian privatization program, where any citizen could purchase vouchers for shares of ownership in Russian companies that were being sold by the government. After he informs Salomon about the program, he is given $1 million to purchase vouchers.

The voucher auction is held in an old, dusty convention hall adjacent to the giant GUM department store. He buys vouchers for Lukoil (a giant oil company) and Rostelecom (the national phone company).

The value of the investments that he makes transforms from $25 million to $125 million in a matter of months, and Browder becomes somewhat of a hero at Salomon Brothers.

Along the way, he meets investment titans like John Templeton and George Soros.

While Salomon Brothers provides him with decent compensation, Browder feels that he is not getting enough recognition for his efforts.

Knowing that he can do the investing on his own, he wants to start his own investment company. With the help of a charismatic Israeli billionaire called Benny Steinmentz, he gets in touch with Edmond Safra, the billionaire owner of the Republic National Bank of New York, who hesitantly listens to his pitch.

With various individuals having pledged amounts totaling $25 million, Browder opens Hermitage Capital for business.

# Chapter 8. Greenacres

It turns out that the $25 million would not immediately materialize. Not many people are willing to invest that much money into the unknown world of investments in Russian companies. Instead, some offer to provide him a salary and bonus while he does the legwork.

But eventually, Steinmetz and Safra together agree to pony up the seed capital plus initial operating expenses. While he is negotiating the investment funds, he meets a beautiful actress, Sabrina, who sweeps him off his feet. They fall in love, and she agrees to fly with him to Moscow.

Browder then begins his international investing career in earnest.

# Chapter 9. Sleeping on the Floor in Davos

In 1996, Bill Browder becomes increasingly concerned about the Russian elections as the prospects of a loss by Boris Yeltsin to hard-line communist Gennady Zyuganov continues to be a possibility; polls show a tight race, and Browder's concern is exacerbated by Yeltsin's deteriorating health. Yeltsin has been a champion of the rise of capitalism in Russia, and Browder is afraid that a communist government under Zyuganov may revert the country to its anti-capitalist system, allowing the government to recover the companies that have been already been privatized, drastically reducing the value of Hermitage's investments in those companies.

Adding to his worries, Edmond Safra asks Browder to create an operations manual for Hermitage, which he must complete seemingly as a prerequisite to receive additional funding for Hermitage.

While running Hermitage, Browder is invited by his friend Mark Holtzman to attend the World Economic Forum in Davos, Switzerland. The WEF is an exclusive event attended by heads of state, economic chiefs of major countries, the world's wealthiest investors, and the heads of the world's top companies.

Holtzman tells Browder that it is an opportunity for Browder to seek out Zyuganov and to get some reassurance that Hermitage can operate as usual in the event of a Zyuganov presidency. He endures sleeping on the floor in a tiny hotel room in Davos to get the opportunity.

However, his sacrifices pay off. He is informed by former Russian Finance Minister Boris Fyodorov that Yeltsin's win over Zyuganov is assured due to the support of billionaire oligarchs like Vladimir Gusinsky and Boris Berezovsky and experienced political operatives like Anatoly Chubai. The icing on the Davos cake, however, is when Zyuganov himself promises Browder that he will not re-nationalize the country in the event that he wins the presidency.

# Chapter 10. Preferred Shares

As Browder is finishing the operations manual for Safra, he still cannot help but feel worried about the elections. Nevertheless, he gets additional operating capital from Edmond Safra, and his Russian operation is now going full bore. He is able to rent a proper office in Moscow and hires competent staff.

Bill is saddened, however, when a pregnant Sabrina tells him that she does not want to go to Moscow at the moment, which is not a good sign given his already difficult long-distance relationship.

As he settles into his new offices, Browder uncovers a gold mine in the frenetic world of Russian de-nationalization: undervalued preferred shares of stock. A case in point is the massive Moscow Oil Refinery, or MNPZ, where preferred shares are trading at up to a discount of 95%. The prices of these preferred shares are discounted much more deeply than common shares of stock, because preferred shares of stock have no voting rights even if they pay up to 40% of their face value in dividends.

Browder notices that Russia is full of these similarly profitable deals, and he makes many investments on these preferred shares. This strategy means that 1996 would be a good year for Bill Browder. After receiving full support from Safra, Browder wisely uses the money entrusted to him.

After a year, the Hermitage fund is up 25%, with better times still to come as Boris Yeltsin wins in the presidential race in a landslide.

To cap off a great year, Browder marries Sabrina on May 26, 1996.

# Chapter 11. Sidanco

The Russian gravy train continues. In August 1996, Browder gets a tip about Sidanco, a big oil company in Western Siberia owned by billionaire Vladimir Potanin.

Four percent of Sidanco's shares are up for sale for $36 million, which is a very steep price at face value. However, when Browder digs deeper, he discovers that the company is really worth $916 million. Still, he feels that the shares may not be truly worth $36 million. As other investment companies have written the company off, his caution is understandable.

After extensive digging to verify the Sidanco reserves and talking to oil industry experts, Browder finds out that Sidanco is as valuable as its more well-known competitor – Lukoil. The only difference is that information about Lukoil is more accessible.

He decides to invest $11 million in Sidanco anyway (roughly 1.2% of Sidanco shares), and is rewarded a few months later when U.K. petroleum giant BP buys the shares for six times their original amount.

# Chapter 12. The Magic Fish

In November 1996, David is born to Bill and Sabrina. It is time to take stock of domestic life and have family vacations in South America to appease an increasingly upset Sabrina, who takes issue with Bill spending most of his time in Moscow away from his family.

While on vacation, he receives disturbing news that Potanin has substantially diluted Hermitage's investment in Sidanco by issuing new shares that reduced the price of existing shares. Bill realizes that there is no apparent financial advantage for this maneuver except that it is a malicious act to "screw" Browder even at great financial losses to Potanin himself. It was one of the strange quirks of the occasionally bewildering Russian psyche – to destroy others even at the expense of destroying yourself.

At this point, some Russians are uncomfortable with Browder's success and influence, and want to make life difficult for him. Browder ends his vacation and returns to Moscow without Sabrina to talk to Boris Morgan, Potanin's adviser. Morgan tells Browder that Potanin will not desist from his dilution tactics.

Bill Browder decides to fight fire with fire. Edmond Safra agrees and sends fifteen armed bodyguards and four armored cars to prepare Bill Browder for his battle against a Russian oligarch.

# Chapter 13. Lawyers, Guns, and Money

Browder's first move is to expose Potanin's tactics to Potanin's foreign business contacts. The tactic is ineffective, as most of the contacts don't even consider Potanin's actions objectionable.

Browder then publicizes Potanin's actions by reporting them to the international newspaper the *Financial Times*. Browder knows that he is now playing dirty, but he realizes that Russia is like a prison yard: if someone comes after you, you need to strike first with the intention to kill.

In response to Browder's public declarations, Potanin says that he considers Browder a foreign intruder. The dilution issue suddenly puts Hermitage Capital in the public eye. Browder then proceeds to report Potanin's actions to the Russian Federal Securities and Exchange Commission, or FSEC, which is the Russian equivalent of the U.S. Securities and Exchange Commission. FSEC'S chairman Dmitry Vasiliev advises Browder to file a formal report if the latter thinks that Potanin has broken Russian laws.

Edmond Safra comes to Browder's "help" by sending his own legal counsel, Sandy Kolman, to Russia to deal with the issue. Safra does so without telling Browder, saying that these legal machinations are out of Browder's league. But before Kolman can tackle Potanin head on, the FSEC orders Potanin to stop the dilution tactics.

Browder not only triumphs over Potanin but over Edmond Safra's lack of belief in Browder's tenacity and skill. Browder, the nobody from the South Side of Chicago, had come to Moscow and beat down a Russian in his own prison yard.

# Chapter 14. Leaving Villa d'Este

After his staredown with the thuggish Potanin, Bill Browder's fortunes are on the upswing. In 1997, his fund records massive gains that surpass Edmond Safra's expectations. However, Safra is worried about the Asian markets and that their continuing decline could affect Russia's economic fortunes.

Browder reassures Safra, believing that the Asian markets are geographically and financially too distant to make an impact on Hermitage's finances. Browder does not scale back on Russia but soon realizes that he has made a terrible decision.

Russia is accruing unsustainable budget deficits that are funded by loans it cannot fully repay. Not even the International Monetary Fund can convince Russia to take a more responsible approach to its national finances. Instead of listening to the IMF, Russia doubles down by increasing the interest rates on its bonds to attract foreign lenders. This has the opposite effect — investors are spooked and they pull their money, sparking a selloff that sends Russian share prices plummeting.

The ensuing stock market crash slashes the value of Hermitage assets by 50%, forcing Browder to devise new strategies to recover the losses. As he is doing so, the IMF infuses $20 billion dollars into Russian coffers to prop up the value of the ruble, which eventually brings back confidence in the Russian stock market. The extra dollars, however, merely serve as bait for the voracious Russian oligarchs, who begin to dump the ruble and purchase more dollars, further driving down the Russian market.

As Hermitage struggles and Browder searches for answers, Sabrina Browder checks in to the Villa d'Este Hotel in the glamourous jetsetter locale of Lake Como in Italy. The room costs $1,200 a night, and Browder reluctantly joins Sabrina on the costly vacation. In the middle of their vacation, Russia announces that it is defaulting on its domestic debt, further driving down share prices.

In a matter of weeks, the value of Hermitage's assets has fallen by 90%, forcing Browder to contemplate his future involvement, or non-involvement, in the Russian markets.

# Chapter 15. And We All Fall Down

In May 1999 Edmond Safra sells his bank, Republic National Bank, to HSBC. It turns out that Safra had personally bet heavily on Russia's bonds without Browder's knowledge.

Safra has divested all of his Russian holdings, including his Hermitage shares, and Browder is crestfallen that Edmond Safra has stopped being his partner. While trying to salvage Hermitage, Browder is also trying to save his fraying marriage to Sabrina. As they are vacationing in Greece in May of 1999, Sabrina Browder suddenly asks Bill for a divorce. He grudgingly agrees and returns to Moscow to try to save Hermitage.

He is returning to a company that now has just $100 million left of its original $1 billion under management. Browder now has no idea with what to do with what was left, given that prospects in Russia have all but disappeared.

In December of that year, Browder receives horrible news: his former partner, Edmond Safra, has died in a fire at his Monaco home.

# Chapter 16. Tuesdays with Morrie

Despite severe investment losses in 1998 and 1999, Bill Browder is committed to staying in Russia to recover what he can from the near collapse of his company. By ruining the Russian economy, the oligarchs have effectively scared off most of the world's investing community; they have run roughshod over every economic asset in sight: oil, gas, minerals, and petroleum. Aside from embezzling, they are also engaging in questionable transfer pricing, dilutions (like what Potanin did), and asset stripping.

At this time, Russia is beset by minority shareholder scandals, where billionaire shareholders trample on minority shareholders by diluting share prices, forcing the latter to sell their shares to the oligarchs for pennies on the dollar.

In January 2000, Browder is asked by the ACC in Moscow to give a speech on corporate governance in Russia with a focus on minority shareholder scandals. He intends to use Yukos, Russia's giant oil company owned by Mikhail Khodorkovsky — at one time considered the richest man in Russia — as his major example. Yukos is the perfect case study because it was involved in many minority shareholder scandals.

Before the seminar, he spots a stunning Russian girl among the predominantly elderly male crowd. She introduced herself as Elena Molokova, a Russian employee of a public relations firm in the United States that advises none other than Mikhail Khodorkovsky.

Elena is a highly educated woman who is all beauty and brains. Despite their cultural and ideological differences, Bill Browder is lovestruck by Elena. After a few tentative dates, she falls for his brilliance and his persistence. Bill Browder had found a new life partner.

# Chapter 17. Stealing Analysis

If Russia was a country paralyzed by official corruption before the fall of the Soviet Union, the union's breakup meant that a new breed of economic predators — the oligarchs — would fleece the country. Despite their depredations, Bill Browder still feels that many companies are still grossly undervalued. He needs to understand the extent of their undervaluation because he has yet to recover 90% of the assets that Hermitage had lost over the past two years. He targets Gazprom, Russia's largest oil and gas company.

He sets out to find out as much as he could about Gazprom, and he discovers that its majority shareholders are stealing major assets like the valuable oil fields that are worth billions of dollars. The problem lies in proving that all this was happening when it is almost impossible to get inside information on public and private companies.

Over the course of this quest, the reality of two main characteristics of Russian life stare him starkly in the face: the massive income gap between the rich and the poor, and the convoluted Russian bureaucracy. This bureaucracy ironically allows Browder to uncover details about Gazprom ownership.

Browder finds out about the bogus asset disposals and who was responsible. He is astounded to learn that Gazprom is still very much undervalued in the marketplace even with the natural resources that remained after the shareholder thefts. He takes a bold step and commits to purchase Gazprom shares despite the unpredictable business environment.

He then publicizes the Gazprom thefts and distributes the information to major media outlets, putting the Gazprom oligarchs on the defensive.

Nevertheless, Bill Browder feels that he still needs to do more. He brings Elena with him to the annual Gazprom shareholders' meeting near Istanbul on June 30, 2001. He is planning to raise a ruckus in the meeting and to continue to expose the rampant cheating that is going on within the company.

He didn't have to. Before the meeting, it is announced that newly elected President Vladimir Putin had fired and replaced Gazprom's CEO, as Russia wanted to avoid further embarrassment. Gazprom becomes more transparent and both its shares and Hermitage's investments went up in value by a hundredfold.

Bill Browder is back on track.

# Chapter 18. Fifty Percent

With his "victory" over Gazprom, Browder decides to make a career revealing thefts and cheating in Russian companies. He decides to go after the national savings bank, Sberbank, as well as a large national electricity company. He feels confident, even as an outsider, that his work is appreciated and important in showing Russia's serious intent to be a major player in international business and finance. Vladimir Putin, for one, wanted to take power from many of the oligarchs who looted the Russian economy for their own selfish gain. Being seen as "Putin's guy" does not hurt at all — Hermitage recovers all of its 1998 losses and then some.

In 2003, however, reality strikes again. Vladimir Khodorovsky is arrested on the orders of Vladimir Putin. His arrest leads to a sharp decline in the Russian markets, which means losses for Browder and Hermitage. Browder believes that this and other arrests are a sign that Putin will not tolerate the oligarchs' political meddling, especially when they align with people who oppose Putin.

More chillingly, Browder learns from sources that Russia is now "50 percent Putin," meaning that any oligarch who wanted to be in Putin's good graces has to turn over about 50% of their wealth over to him. As he gets the oligarchs to fall in line, Putin is no longer interested in exposing the corruption in which the oligarchs are involved. They could be as dirty and corrupt as they wanted, as long as they contribute and are loyal to Putin.

This is an ominous development. Since Bill Browder is in a vigorous crusade against the oligarchs' misdeeds, he is now seen as a threat to Putin's own interests and aspirations. His expulsion from Russia in November 2005 means that he is now a persona non grata in the Land of the Czars.

# Chapter 19. A Threat to National Security

After being unceremoniously shipped back to London, Browder is eager to find out why the expulsion happened. More importantly, he wants to find a way to get back to Russia to Hermitage, which at the time was managing $4.5 billion USD in assets.

He meets a representative of the Foreign Affairs office in Moscow, who tells him that even the British ambassador to Russia does not know that Browder was kicked out of the country. A few days later, Browder finds out via a fax from the Russian Foreign Ministry that Russia considers him to a threat to national security.

# Chapter 20. Vogue Café

On December 15, 2005, just a few weeks after being kicked out of Russia, Sabrina gives birth to a daughter, Jessica. This joy is quickly doused when less than a month later, the British foreign office in Russia is approached by the Russian FSB, the Federal Security Office, and the successor to the once terrifying KGB. The FSB warns the British foreign service to cease its investigation of the Browder case.

Further probing convinces Browder and his friends that the decision to keep him out of Russia comes from way up high in the Russian government, most probably from Vladimir Putin. Browder believes that Putin has been fed misinformation about him and that there should be some way for him to clear the air and get back in Putin's good graces.

He asks Vadim, his assistant in Russia, to look for an inside track to Putin. Instead, he is told that Browder's case has been left with the FSB, which is now looking into closing Hermitage and seizing its assets. Vadim is advised that his life may be in danger, so he leaves Russia for London.

They get a sympathetic ear in Arkady Dvorkovich, a Putin adviser, who says that expelling Browder and seizing Hermitage is bad for the Russian image abroad. Things get much worse when the news media reports that Browder's visa has been revoked and that he is expelled from Russia. Instead of backing down, Russia saves face and digs in, meaning that it will try to keep Browder barred from Russia forever.

# Chapter 21. The G8

The news from Russia convinces Browder that he should focus not on preserving Hermitage's existence in Russia, but on getting it out with its assets fairly intact. His biggest challenge is to divest his asset portfolio of Russian securities without alerting the Russian authorities. He is able to find an inconspicuous individual broker who successfully sells Hermitage's portfolio of over 4 billion dollars within a few weeks, by surreptitiously selling securities in 100-million-dollar chunks.

Browder's next challenge is to retain the investors who kept their Hermitage assets because they valued Browder's Russian connections. In a few months, by March 2006, these investors withdraw 20% of the fund's assets. Browder knows that his revoked visa would continue to cause his fund to lose money.

His spirits are revived when he finds out that British Prime Minister Tony Blair plans to talk to Putin about Browder's visa issue during the G8 summit in St. Petersburg, Russia. During a question-and-answer session, Putin is directly asked why Browder's visa was revoked. Putin says that the visa was revoked because Browder is considered an enemy of the state, and that Russia is pursuing criminal charges against him and Hermitage.

# Chapter 22. The Raids

The next redemption date for Hermitage's investors is August 25, 2006; and on that date, Hermitage clients withdraw another 30% of their investments. Clearly, Hermitage needed to diversify its investor base outside of Russia.

Browder figures that his knack for finding undervalued companies could be applied to other countries as well. He transforms his company into "Hermitage Global," and begins investing in countries like Thailand, Brazil, and Turkey.

Browder brings Elena to the World Economic Forum in Davos in January 2007, and Elena suggests that he meet with Russian Prime Minister Dmitri Medvedev, who was giving a talk at the forum. Medvedev listens to Browder's story and tells him that he will see what he can do about Browder's revoked visa.

On February 19, Browder receives a response from Russia's Federal Border Service that agents would like to meet with Browder personally to discuss his visa issues. Fearful that he would be thrown in jail if he went back to Moscow, Browder ignores the message. After all, his global business has already raised $625 million and things are looking up.

On June 24, 2007, he gets a call from Russia informing him that the Hermitage office in Moscow is being ransacked and searched by 25 Russian officers. Not only do the officers take away almost everything from the office, they also send one of his staff to the hospital after a severe beating. Browder now knows that his entreaty to Medvedev has only made matters worse, and this is just the beginning of an all-out war against him.

# Chapter 23. Department K

The Russian government files a $44 million fraud case against the president of one of the companies in Hermitage's Russian portfolio, and arrests Hermitage's chief operating officer Ivan Chersakov.

Browder immediately hires two Russian attorneys, Sergei Magnitsky and Eduard Khayretdino, to not only defend against the lawsuit but to find out who is behind the raid of Hermitage's Moscow office.

After some furious digging, the attorneys find out that the raids were engineered by the feared Department K of the FSB, the Russian government's economic counterespionage unit. Known for its secrecy, Department K has also been suspected of sending assassins to kill Russia's enemies.

# Chapter 24. "But Russian Stories Never Have Happy Endings"

In the midst of all his troubles, Browder and Elena's second daughter Veronica is born in 2007. Browder finally tells her that Department K is after him.

Instead of panicking, Elena suggests that they go on their planned vacation. While on vacation, he receives news that the offices of Credit Suisse, ING Bank, and HSBC are being searched and raided because agents were looking for anything linking the banks to Browder and Hermitage. Fortunately, they find nothing unusual.

While on a trip in South Korea, Browder learns that a Saint Petersburg court has just issued a judgment of $71 million against one of Hermitage's investment companies and was looking to collect on the judgment. Browder later finds out that Hermitage is a victim of a "Russian raider attack," where someone takes beneficial ownership of a company without the real or original owners knowing about it. The new "owners" then proceed to conduct all sorts of illegal activity, and the original owners would be left to deal with the fallout and accusations.

Someone had spent a lot of money to orchestrate the attack but had come out empty-handed because there was no money to be collected from Hermitage. During these terrible times, not losing is tantamount to winning, but as it has been said, there are no happy endings with any Russian story.

# Chapter 25. High-Pitched Jamming Equipment

Being on the defensive did not sit well with Browder, so he goes on the legal offensive. He hires a Russian defense attorney, Eduard Khayretdinov, a former judge and police investigator.

Eduard quickly goes after Interior Ministry officer, Colonel Artem Kuznetsov, and the lead FSB investigator on the Hermitage case, Pavel Karpov. Eduard pressures Karpov into admitting that it was Kuznetov's initiative to raid Hermitage, but these pressure tactics would only anger the Russians.

Back in London, Browder is invited to a meeting with Igor Sagiryan, the president of Renaissance Capital, one of Browder's earliest contacts in Russia. Browder is later informed that Sagiryan wanted to liquidate companies that were stolen from Hermitage. With such a strange request, Browder agreed to meet with Sagiryan, but only after he is outfitted with listening devices so that his attorneys and British officials could eavesdrop on the conversation.

During the meeting, Sagiryan asks Browder about liquidating the companies, which is unusual because Hermitage did not own the companies to which Sagiryan was referring. After the unproductive meeting, Browder and his team find out that the Russians have used jamming devices that prevented the recorder from working properly. This means that Sagiryan is probably a spy and Russian operatives are close by.

Things would only get worse — a few months later, Browder is formally charged with tax evasion in Russia.

# Chapter 26. The Riddle

To help unravel *why* he is being harassed by the Russians, Browder believes the key to this riddle is finding out *who* is involved.

Knowing that a lawsuit in a major Moscow court would raise a lot of flags, Browder, and his legal team go instead to a small city in the remote Republic of Tatarstan to determine who stole his companies and committed crimes under his name. They discover that a total of about $1 billion in lawsuits has been filed against the companies that were stolen from Hermitage.

They find out that the perpetrators had played a shell game of moving the domiciles, or official addresses, of the stolen companies from one obscure city to another. Browder and his cohorts get another surprise: an old business nemesis named Kuznetsov has been assigned to their case. Despite this setback, they continue to research until identities and agendas slowly begin to surface.

Finally, they ascertain the real reason why their companies, practically stripped of their assets and generating no revenue, were being registered. The perpetrators were setting up a mechanism where they could get refunds from taxes paid by these companies during the time that Hermitage owned them. At over $200 million, it would be the largest tax refund in Russian history, and Browder was intent on keeping it from happening.

# Chapter 27. DHL

Certain that he would get sympathy from outside Russia for the blatant tax fraud being perpetrated against him, Browder goes public with what he had uncovered. In July 2008, he has a 45-minute interview with Russia's leading independent radio station Echo Moscow to explain the details of the tax fraud.

He expects public uproar and a defensive response from Russia. He gets no response from Moscow until his Russian attorneys tell him that a DHL package received at the Moscow Hermitage offices was intercepted and seized by Russian authorities, who ask DHL where the package came from, and they get the stunning response: the package came from Browder's Hermitage offices in London. Russian agents had obviously fabricated the DHL package and doubtlessly stuffed the package with incriminating information that they would then say came from Browder.

The incident shows Browder that the Russians will stop at nothing to get to him. He begins to worry about his staff and his lawyers in Russia; fearing for their safety, he warns them that they need to leave Russia. Vladimir and Eduard receive a summons, and Eduard is the first to act. He takes his wife and goes into hiding in Moscow as they devise a plan to leave Russia.

On the day that he is supposed to answer his summons, Vladimir slips past Russian security and escapes to Milan, Italy. It is now up to Eduard to craft his own escape.

# Chapter 28. Khabarovsk

With Vladimir's escape, the Russians get hotter on the trail of Eduard. Eduard, through a series of surreptitious moves from one location to another, is able to get under the radar of the Russian authorities. But Eduard knows that his ultimate salvation lies in leaving Russia; he is getting tired of the subterfuge, including hiding in the back seat of a car.

He finds an ally in Mikhail, whom he had saved from some legal tussle years earlier. Mikhail tells Eduard that his best chance of escaping is to first go to the remote city of Khabarovsk, which is 500 miles away from Moscow, where Mikhail can shelter Eduard almost indefinitely until Eduard figures out an escape from Russia. After a series of close calls, Eduard finally secures a flight to London from South Korea.

However, one valuable person still remains in Russia; Sergei Magnitsky, the 36-year-old lawyer, is absolutely sure that he could be exonerated by working through the Russian legal system. Browder and company know that this is a pipe dream at best.

# Chapter 29. The Ninth Commandment

Having lost Vladimir and Eduard, the Russian authorities begin to concentrate their efforts on Sergei Magnitsky. On November 24, 2008, they search Sergei's home, confiscate his personal effects, and arrest him in front of his wife and children. Confident that he would beat the rap, Magnitsky tells his family that he would be back soon. Having learned of Sergei's arrest, Browder asks his Russian and European contacts to help secure Sergei's release from prison.

However, it soon becomes apparent that Sergei is not going to have it easy. Victor Voronin, the head of the feared Department K of the FSB, is personally assigned to Sergei's case. In addition, nine investigators are assigned to his case instead of the usual two. They plan to pressure Sergei until he retracts his charges against Karpov and Kuznetsov. Sergi refuses, and is moved to a harsher prison and deprived of contact with his family.

Over the course of 2009, Browder does all he can to help Sergei, whose fate is unknown as the Russians successfully keep his existence under wraps. In October 2009, Browder goes public with Sergei's story, seeks the assistance of international human rights groups, and even posts a YouTube video. However, their efforts are largely unsuccessful as the Russians hold their ground.

Unknown to everyone, Sergei's physical condition is worsening; he is constantly refused medical attention as he steadfastly refuses to cooperate with Russian authorities.

# Chapter 30. November 16, 2009

In October 2009, Browder receives troubling news on his way back from lobbying the U.S. government for help on Sergei's behalf. The Russian government has filed a tax evasion case against Browder and Sergei, and that they are facing a sentence of six years. Russia issues an arrest order and asks Interpol to issue a Red Notice for Browder's arrest in a foreign jurisdiction.

The conviction garners media attention, and Browder realizes that he has a target on his back; the Russians are willing to get to him by any means necessary.

On November 16, 2009, Sergei's attorney visits Sergei in prison. Prison authorities refuse the lawyer and finally tell him that Sergei is too sick to see anyone, having been left untreated with cholecystitis, gallstones, and pancreatitis. When Magnitsky demands more medical attention, he is cuffed to his bed and beaten with batons. A few hours after Sergei's attorney asks to see him, Sergei Magnitsky dies in his cell.

# Chapter 31. The Katyn Principle

The Katyn forest was the site of one of the most audacious cover-ups by the Russians during World War II. A Russian official, Vasili Mikhailovich Blokhin, had 7,000 prisoners of war summarily executed and their bodies transported to the Katyn forest. Up until the 1990s, the Russians insisted that the Germans were responsible. This cover-up has since been called the Katyn Principle.

The Russians apply this principle to Sergei Magnitsky's death. They insist that Sergei died while under hospital care and that he was subjected to constant medical attention. Browder has Magnitsky's death and subsequent cover-up publicized, and Russia seems to take heed. Prime Minister Medvedev orders an investigation which leads to the firing of nineteen soldiers who were not even assigned to the prison in which Magnitsky died.

Browder knows that it was all a cover-up, and he vows to involve the United States, the last remaining bastion of justice.

# Chapter 32. Kyle Parker's War

Browder goes to Washington, D.C. to solicit the help of the United States in his crusade of justice for Sergei. His first point of contact is an international rights attorney, Jonathan Winer, who tells him about Proclamation 7550, which was passed in 2004 during the George W. Bush administration.

Proclamation 7550 imposes restrictions and even cancellations of visas issued to foreign nationals as a sanction against their home countries. While it is a harsh sanction with severe diplomatic repercussions, Browder wants to go big and get loud.

Browder is initially stonewalled by the Office of Russian Affairs in the U.S. State Department. However, through a series of contacts, he meets Kyle Parker of the U.S. Helsinki Commission. The Commission is a part of a multinational effort to combat human rights abuses all over the world. Parker lends a sympathetic ear and tells Browder that he can raise the issue of Magnitsky with Secretary of State Hillary Clinton through Maryland Senator Ben Cardin.

# Chapter 33. Russell 241

In March 2010, Kyle Parker convinces the office of Senator Ben Cardin to send a letter to Secretary Clinton asking for visa sanctions against Russians who were involved in the "crime" against Sergei Magnitsky.

Ben Cardin's letter is finally posted on the website of the U.S. Helsinki Commission, along with the pictures of Kuznetsov and Karpov, a list of sixty Russians involved in the death of Sergei, and a detailed description of the events that led to his death. While the Russians are apoplectic, the U.S. State Department remains unmoved by the onrush of revelations.

On May 6, 2010, a hearing on the case is conducted by a U.S. Human Rights Commission of the U.S. Congress under Congressman Tom Lantos. Browder gives an impassioned presentation of the Sergei saga and asks that a U.S. law be passed to punish people involved in human rights abuses all over the world.

After his 8-minute speech, Browder gets a warm response for those in attendance. On September 21, 2010, Browder gets an appointment with a key member of the U.S. Senate, John

McCain, who was himself once a prisoner who was subjected to torture. In McCain's chambers in the Russell 241 Room in the U.S. Capitol, McCain promises to help pass the Magnitsky Act.

# Chapter 34. Russian Untouchables

During his trips to and from Washington D.C. and London, Browder continues to hear stories about Kuznetsov and Karpov, and how Sergei Magnitsky was not their only victim. Browder decides that as part of his crusade of justice for Sergei, he wants to find out as much as he can about Kuznetsov and Karpov.

One of the astounding things that Browder discovers is that Kuznetsov has an extravagant lifestyle and possessions that should have been only for the truly wealthy. He has luxurious properties under his and his relatives' names, owns expensive cars, and takes expensive foreign trips with his wife. Browder estimates that Kusnetsov would have had to work 145 years in his current position to amass that kind of money.

To expose the infamous duo, Browder publishes a YouTube video series called "Untouchables", and launches a website (www.russian-untouchables.com) which maintains that people like Kuznetsov and Karpov could do anything they want in Russia so long as they carry out the government's sinister directives.

While Browder knows that Kuznetsov and Karpov are untouchable, he figures that public opinion could influence them in ways that Russians could not.

# Chapter 35. The Swiss Accounts

While on vacation with his son in August 2010, Browder receives documents stating that the husband of Olga Stepanova, the lady that signed the refund checks in the tax refund fiasco, had received millions of dollars in his Swiss bank account. The sender of the documents, a certain "Alejandro Sanches," agrees to meet with Browder in London to provide more details.

On August 27, 2010, Browder meets with Sanches, whose real name is Alexander Perepilichnyy, in London. During the meeting, Perepilichnyy produces reports from Credit Suisse stating that Vladen Stepanova deposited 7.1 million euros over a two-month period in 2008 via a Cypriot-based company registered under Vladen's name.

Over the next few weeks, Perepilichnyy continues to provide information about Stepanova before finally admitting that he once worked for the Stepanovas and had moved money for them. He reveals that the reason he is disclosing this information is because the Stepanovas are accusing him of stealing from them. These accusations coincide with the decline in value of the investments in the wake of the worldwide economic downturn in 2008.

Despite the juicy nature of the information, Browder is suspicious. After all, Alexander Perepilichnyy may very well be an FSB agent sent to sow disinformation.

# Chapter 36. The Tax Princess

Browder proceeds with caution regarding the Perepilichnyy documents. He continues to uncover information that seems to solidify the case against Olga Stepanova.

While Browder is getting verification from Credit Suisse to release his YouTube video on Stepanova, the Russians try to whitewash Stepanova's involvement by convicting someone else. In this instance, it is ex-felon Vyacheslav Khlebnikov, who they convict for his alleged role in the tax-rebate fraud; because of him, tax officials such as Stepanova were misled in paying out the fraudulent tax refunds.

This is too much for Browder. Before Credit Suisse could verify the incriminatory information on Stepanova, Browder releases his YouTube video on April 20, 2011. The early release achieves some of its desired results. The Stepanovas are now being harangued by the foreign media, and the Swiss attorneys not only freeze the Stepanovas' Swiss bank accounts but also launch a money-laundering investigation against the couple.

# Chapter 37. Sausage Making

As the Magnitsky Bill nears a vote in the U.S. Congress, the Russians counter by not only bestowing a "Best Police Investigator" award on Pavel Karpov but by also having Interior Ministry spokesperson Irina Dudukina present a falsified report stating that Sergei Magnitsky was the beneficiary of the $230 million tax fraud.

Despite the growing support for the proposed Magnitsky Bill, the U.S. State Department initially snubs the bill by claiming that current laws already exist to punish foreign countries that were guilty of human rights abuses. A new law would be redundant and would need to pass through the sausage-making machine that is the U.S. Congress. The passage of legislation in Congress is about as mysterious, labyrinthine, and even as disgusting as sausage making, a process through which the Magnitsky Bill has to maneuver.

The bill first has to be approved by the Foreign Relations Committee. It then has to pass through the Senate Finance Committee, which at the moment is struggling to repeal a Jackson-Vanik Act implementing economic sanctions on countries that were involved in the Soviet-era persecution of Russian Jews.

Initially, Senator John Kerry is hesitant to append his name to the bill, which would actually help his agenda when he took over the State Department (as Hillary Clinton plans to step down to run for U.S. President). Eventually, however, Senator Kerry gets on board, and the Magnitsky Bill train starts rolling again.

# Chapter 38. The Malkin Delegation

In a last-ditch effort to derail the Magnitsky Bill, which now has the support of the U.S. government, the Russians send a delegation led by a billionaire parliamentarian named Vitaly Malkin and four members of the Federation Council. The Council is Russia's upper chamber of Parliament (its version of the U.S. Senate).

Malkin is considered a persona non grata by Canada for being involved in a group that committed so-called "transnational" crimes, so his job to lobby the U.S. government on behalf of accused criminals is an ironic choice. Malkin and his team conduct meetings with high-level U.S. government officials, but fail to fool anyone with their rehashing of old lies and invention of new ones. The delegation's words are so bad that even the Russian government disavows all of their testimonies.

But the Russians are not done. When Browder returns to London after the Malkin misfire, he gets a formal notice that he is being sued for libel by Pavel Karpov. But that is not all that the Russians have in store. On November 16, 2012, Browder learns that the Russian who divulged the Swiss bank accounts of Olga Stepanova, Alexander Perepilichnyy, had dropped dead while jogging in front of his house in the British town of Surrey.

# Chapter 39. Justice for Sergei

Still digesting the news of Alexander Perepilichnyy's death, Browder learns that the Magnitsky Bill has been approved by the U.S. House of Representatives with a vote of 365-43. When he gets home, he finds Elena distressed over the death of Alexander Perepilichnyy. The couple feel that his death was neither accidental nor natural. After all, the Russians are known to publicly assassinate political enemies in other countries.

Browder asks his London lawyer, Mary, to contact the local police to learn as much as possible about Perepilichnyy's death. He is worried that there would be a long delay in determining the true cause of Perepilichnyy's death, as the initial tests have come back inconclusive.

Meantime, the U.S. Senate has not yet voted on the Magnitsky bill, which has stalled because some senators want to change its scope. The delays in the Magnitsky Bill vote and the death of Perepilichnyy so close to home begin to worry Browder.

However, on December 6, 2012, all of Browder's work and the sacrifices of Sergei Magnitsky and his family finally pay off. The U.S. Senate votes in favor of the Magnitsky Bill by an overwhelming vote of 92-4.

# Chapter 40. Humiliator, Humiliatee

Vladimir Putin does not take the passage of the Magnitsky Bill sitting down, although his retaliatory ideas like seizing $3.5 billion of Citibank's assets in Russia could not be implemented. He needs to think of something that would not necessarily affect the Americans economically, but would still catch their attention.

On December 11, 2012, it finally comes. Browder finds out that the Russian parliament is considering an adoption ban of Russian children by Americans. The move actually hurts the Russians more, since 60,000 of its impoverished children have found much better lives in the United States.

Despite the outcry in Russia, Putin stands his ground; during a press conference, he not only rehashes the lies about Sergei Magnitsky, but mentions Browder by name, claiming that Browder is a criminal that was being represented by Magnitsky, who had significant financial interests in the alleged criminal activities of which Browder was accused.

The Russian parliament, in lockstep with their president, votes for the ban on U.S. adoptions of American children, including the 300 or so babies that are already in the process of moving to the United States. A huge demonstration is staged by over 50,000 irate Russians in Moscow. They call the Russian parliament and Putin "baby haters".

Putin then goes after the architect of the accursed Magnitsky affair — Bill Browder.

# Chapter 41. Red Notice

While attending the World Economic Forum in Davos in January 2013, Browder is told that Prime Minister Medvedev of Russia apparently uttered veiled threats against Browder. Browder is forced to increase his personal security as he considers it unusual that a prime minister would go to the extent of mentioning an enemy by name.

In March 2013, Russia trials Magnitsky and Browder *in absentia* for tax evasion and fraud. In addition to this, Browder is charged with other crimes of theft and economic sabotage. Two public defenders that are initially commissioned to defend Browder and Magnitsky stop going to the proceedings as the verdict seems all but set in stone. Magnitsky and Browder are convicted for their crimes, and the Russian authorities order Browder's arrest.

In the middle of May, Browder is informed that a Red Notice had been issued for his arrest by the Interpol, which means that he will be extradited to Russia if he is ever brought into custody by any country's law enforcement agency. Browder fights the Red Notice, and on May 24, 2013, Interpol informs Browder that it has rejected Russia's application for his arrest.

The rejection angers the Russians and Putin. On July 11, 2013, a judge in Russia sentences Browder to nine years in prison for fraud. It is a foregone conclusion anyway, as Browder was in the clear anywhere in the world, except for Russia.

# Chapter 42. Feelings

Bill Browder says that the most powerful emotion that he had with his almost twenty years of experience with Russia, is one of sadness, especially because of the death of Sergei Magnitsky, which he said would never have happened if he had never made his acquaintance. Magnitsky's death is Browder's one biggest regret in life — not his business failures, and not even his first marriage.

Through all his successes in college and investment banking, most of what matters to Browder now is how he can make sure that the spirit of the Magnitsky Act is kept alive. This is especially relevant in today's world when international borders seem to be blurring because of the dizzying advances in technology.

He has a deep sense of pride and accomplishment that his revelations about Magnitsky's death have led to changes in not only how the international community perceives Russia but also in changes within Russia itself, especially with regards to prisoners' rights and orphaned children. Even while Russia does not appear to have softened its stance against Bill Browder — in fact, he doesn't relinquish the idea Russia might have him murdered one day — it appears that Russia may have softened its own positions within its borders.

When the European Parliament unanimously approves its own measures against human rights abuses against the 30 or so people that were involved in Magnitsky's death, he says that getting justice for Sergei is more satisfying than any financial success that he ever and would ever have. He adds that it feels good that justice still exists in a world full of injustice.

# Conclusion

As an autobiographer, Bill Browder doesn't tell us what a singularly outstanding individual he is, but we cannot help but be impressed at his credentials even before he talks about starting Hermitage Capital.

He was a gold-plated individual almost from Day 1, blessed with the genes of remarkable parents. He attended an expensive boarding school, went to University of Chicago, Stanford, and his first job after college was with two of the biggest and most reputable consulting groups: Bain Capital and the Boston Consulting Group.

But it's apparent from the first seven chapters that Browder focuses, appreciates, and treasures the important people in his life, including the villains. He gives as detailed descriptions of these people as possible, including their height, eye color, manner of dress, and distinctive mannerisms. He tries to put the reader as close to these people as if we are right there with him and to help the reader get as close to his own experiences as he can.

There are many reasons to admire Bill Browder, even as people who despise crass capitalism may frown upon what he did. Like the corrupt oligarchs and politicians who took advantage of communist Russia's demise in the 1990s, Bill Browder made a lot of money as he preyed on the ignorance of the vast majority of Russians, the inefficiencies of the Russian economy, and the deficiencies of Russian governmental authority and regulation. In this way, he is not much different from Boris Bereshovsky, Alexander Abramovich, and even Vladimir Putin, who used influence, money, and inside information to enrich themselves. One major thing, however, separates Bill Browder from the other vultures during the privatization spree in the late 1990s, which was his apparent aversion to criminal activity — Browder has always played by the rules.

Today, Bill Browder seems to be none the worse for wear from his Russian experience. There is no doubt that he occasionally still looks over his shoulders, fearful that Vladimir Putin and the Russians may have one last surprise for him. He still has Hermitage Capital and is but one person in a growing group of people who are both fearful of and angry at an increasingly aggressive and meddlesome Russia.

His last hurrah in *Red Notice* was to allow Magnitsky's family to revel in applause and appreciation as the European parliament unanimously passed its own version of the Magnitsky Act. It reminded Bill Browder and all those who share in his crusade, that any acclaim and honor belongs not to him but to the victims to whom Browder now dedicates a big part of his life.

# FREE BONUSES

**P.S. Is it okay if we overdeliver?**

Here at Readtrepreneur Publishing, we believe in overdelivering way beyond our reader's expectations. Is it okay if we overdeliver?

Here's the deal, we're going to give you an extremely condensed PDF summary of the book which you've just read and much more…

What's the catch? We need to trust you… You see, we want to overdeliver and in order for us to do that, we've to trust our reader to keep this bonus a secret to themselves? Why? Because we don't want people to be getting our exclusive PDF summaries even without buying our books itself. Unethical, right?

Ok. Are you ready?

Firstly, remember that your book is code: "**READ71**".

Next, visit this link: **http://bit.ly/exclusivepdfs**

Everything else will be self explanatory after you've visited: **http://bit.ly/exclusivepdfs**.

We hope you'll enjoy our free bonuses as much as we enjoyed preparing it for you!

# Summary:

# Rich Dad Poor Dad

## By: Robert Kiyosaki

**Proudly Brought to you by:**

# Legal & Disclaimer

agree to hold harmless the Author from and against any damages, costs, and expenses, including any legal fees potentially resulting from the application of any of the information provided by this guide. This disclaimer applies to any damages or injury caused by the use and application, whether directly or indirectly, of any advice or information presented, whether for breach of contract, tort, negligence, personal injury, criminal intent, or under any other cause of action.

You agree to accept all risks of using the information presented inside this book. You need to consult a professional medical practitioner in order to ensure you are both able and healthy enough to participate in this program.

# Table of Contents

# The Book at a Glance

This book presents a chapter by chapter summary of *Rich Dad, Poor Dad*, a book based on the story of the narrator and author, Robert T. Kiyosak, a businessman and investor.

Robert Kiyosaki has two fathers. He calls his biological father the poor dad and refers to his childhood best friend's father as his rich dad. Both dads taught him how to achieve success, but provided disparate goals and approaches. At a young age, Robert was able to discern which dad's set of financial principles and ideas made more sense.

The author compares his two fathers in terms of their financial concepts, practices, and dynamism. He shares six major lessons his rich dad taught him and provides the philosophies and action tips that can help his readers achieve financial success.

Here's an overview of this book:

**Introduction:**

Sharon Lecther, a CPA and co-author of Robert Kiyosaki, explains in detail why there is a need for new ideas and approaches that can help children attain financial literacy.

## Chapter 1    Rich Dad, Poor Dad

This chapter highlights the comparison between Kiyosaki's two dads in terms of their academic background, financial principles, insights, and ideals. He decided that his rich dad made more financial sense and he began to take lessons from him when he was nine years old. His rich dad mentored him for 30 years.

## Chapter 2    The Rich Don't Work for Money

Robert and Mike were childhood best friends who came from almost similar socio-economic backgrounds. They both felt that they didn't belong to their school where the town's elite send their children. They were hurt by being left out and reminded frequently that they were poor.

The two resolved to get rich and tried a nickel counterfeiting scheme which they realized was illegal. Robert's father advised them to ask Mike's father to teach them how to get rich. Mike's dad gave them a taste of the Rat Race by making them work at his grocery store for three hours at a miserly pay. Kiyosaki felt exploited and cheated. After three weeks, he demanded a raise and threatened to quit.

Mike's father explained his way of teaching a lesson, and asked Mike and his friend to work for free. The boys did as they were told until they became tired of the arrangement. Rich dad asked them to choose between the lesson and a huge pay hike. Both boys decided to learn the lesson. The lesson was to move oneself out of the Rat Race and have people working for you instead of you working hard to put huge money in another person's pocket and some crumbs for your own wallet.

**Chapter 3        Why Teach Financial Literacy?**

Kiyosaki discusses the second lesson he learned from his rich dad. He explains why financial education is vital. He teaches the foundation of financial literacy, which is the ability to distinguish an asset from a liability. He introduces simple cash flow diagrams to make it easier for his readers to grasp profound accounting and financial concepts. In this chapter, Kiyosaki explains why the rich are getting richer and why the middle class are struggling.

**Chapter 4        Mind Your Business**

Kiyosaki lightly introduces the strategy of real estate investing citing McDonald's as example. He says that people should strive to be their own boss and manage their own business instead of working hard for their employer. This is the third lesson.

The author expounds on asset building. He reveals his investment preferences and shares his strategies.

## Chapter 5    The History of Taxes and the Power of Corporations

Kiyosaki states that the poor and middle class allow corporations to manipulate them while the rich have the financial savvy to make corporations work for them. The rich know how to exploit the powers of the corporation to grow and protect their assets. The author discusses the tax advantages of a corporate setup and how the rich use these privileges to reduce their taxes.

## Chapter 6    The Rich Invent Money

Kiyosaki explains how self-doubt and fears suppresses a person's innate talents. He tells his readers that in real life, individuals with bravado or guts are the ones who are more likely to succeed. He believes that people should create money and not simply wait around for luck or opportunities. He advises people to capitalize on the knowledge of others by hiring individuals who are more skilled and intelligent than them.

### Chapter 7  Work to Learn, Don't Work for Money

The author discusses the skills that people need to develop in order to achieve financial success. He tells how wealthy families give money away and contrasts them to poor people who insist that charity starts at home.

### Chapter 8  Overcoming Obstacles

Kiyosaki lists five personality traits that are hindering people from getting rich and recommends ways to overcome them.

### Chapter 9  Getting Started

In this chapter, the author provides ten strategies to build personal wealth.

### Chapter 10  Still Want More? Here are Some to Do's

Kiyosaki gives more action tips to supplement the strategies in the previous chapter.

### Epilogue  College Education for $7,000

The author tells his readers how it is possible to pay for a child's college education with only $7,000. He uses a friend's successful investment strategy to demonstrate this point.

# FREE BONUSES

### P.S. Is it okay if we overdeliver?

Here at Readtrepreneur Publishing, we believe in overdelivering way beyond our reader's expectations. Is it okay if we overdeliver?

Here's the deal, we're going to give you an extremely condensed PDF summary of the book which you've just read and much more...

What's the catch? We need to trust you... You see, we want to overdeliver and in order for us to do that, we've to trust our reader to keep this bonus a secret to themselves? Why? Because we don't want people to be getting our exclusive PDF summaries even without buying our books itself. Unethical, right?

Ok. Are you ready?

Firstly, remember that your book is code: "**READ72**".

Next, visit this link: **http://bit.ly/exclusivepdfs**

Everything else will be self explanatory after you've visited: **http://bit.ly/exclusivepdfs**.

We hope you'll enjoy our free bonuses as much as we enjoyed preparing it for you!

# Introduction: There is a Need

Sharon Lechter and Robert Kiyosaki co-authored the book *Rich Dad, Poor Dad.* Sharon Lechter is a CPA who graduated with honors from Florida State University in 1976. She was employed by a top 8 accounting firm and was anticipating a long career and early retirement like most people. She is married to Mike, another career-oriented person who came from a similar family and educational background. They have three children.

Sharon and Mike both have successful careers but were unsatisfied with the way their retirement funds were growing only through their own efforts. Her belief in the traditional career and life path she had known since childhood was shaken by one of the conversations she had with her son in.

Sharon's son was disillusioned about school and was complaining about being forced to study subjects that he felt were not useful in real life. Sharon explained that he needs good grades to qualify for college. She told him that a college degree is indispensable if he wants to land a good job and get rich.

Her son replied that he didn't need a college degree to get rich. He cited the richest people of the time such as Madonna, Michael Jordan, and Bill Gates who achieved their great wealth despite dropping out of school. He told her of a mentally-challenged baseball pitcher who made $4 million annually.

Sharon realized that although the times have changed, she was still handing out the same advice she had heard from her parents. Academic achievements no longer guarantee success but this fact seems to have gone unnoticed by everyone other than their children.

Her son told her further that he didn't want to live like his parents who work hard and make huge money, only to be taxed and saddled with debts. He was aware that there is no such thing as job security nowadays and that today's college graduates are earning less than what his parents' generation earned after graduating. He was aware that he can't depend on company pension and Social Security for retirement. He told her mom that he needs new solutions.

Sharon realized that she also needed new solutions. Her

parents' career ideas could be ill-fitting for people born in a fast moving world. She knew she had to find new approaches to steer her children to the right educational path. Sharon expressed her concern for the school's deficiency in providing financial education. She laments that the absence of financial literacy and a clear understanding of money make today's youth ill-prepared for the real world.

Sharon was in search of a program that can help her teach her children about finances, when she was introduced to Robert Kiyosaki, an investor and businessman. Kiyosaki was then applying for a patent on CASHFLOW, an educational product he was developing. Mike, her husband, was impressed with the new product. The couple and their daughter, a college freshman, participated in a trial for the prototype. About fifteen people participated in the test.

CASHFLOW turned out to be the product Sharon had been searching for. The game looked similar to a Monopoly board except that it features two tracks. The inside track was called the Rat Race. The player has to escape the inside track and move over to the "Fast Track", the outer track.

Kiyosaki describes the "Fast Track" as a simulation of the way the rich plays. He gave a longer definition of the "Rat Race" by describing how generations of hardworking people would continue pursuing the same formula of studying hard, getting a college degree, and settling into a secure career or job.

Robert described how an average couple is trapped into a Rat Race because of their growing need for money. They end up working for their company's owner, the government, the mortgagor bank, and credit card companies. The couple gives the same advice they heard from their parents to their children and work hard for the rest of their life. They remain clueless about how money works and learn about it from people who are taking advantage of their ignorance.

To escape the "Rat Race", a person has to demonstrate proficiency in investing and accounting. Kiyosaki made these two difficult subjects seem entertaining and thrilling.

Her familiarity with financial statements gave Sharon a distinct advantage over the rest of the players. She was the first and only player to move out of the "Rat Race". She was also able to impart important concepts to her daughter and the other members of her group, which included an entrepreneur, a computer programmer, and a banker. Sharon was perturbed with her realization that these people have very little knowledge about investing and accounting. She thought about the number of people who are struggling with their finances simply because they never learned these subjects.

Sharon's daughter enjoyed the game and was happy to have learned about money and investing. She expressed her realization that she can choose a career based on what she wanted to do and not for security, compensation, or benefits. She knew that by learning what the game aims to teach, she can follow her heart's desire and didn't have to take up a course just to meet the job skill requirements of companies.

Sharon and Mike met with Kiyosaki and his wife a week later. They both realized that they have many things in common. Their discussion ranged from sports to socio-economic issues. They talked about how Americans have little or no retirement funds and the dwindling funds of Medicare and Social Security. They wondered if people knew about the risks of depending on pension plans.

Sharon observed that Kiyosaki's foremost concern was the widening gap between the rich and the poor. Kiyosaki is well aware that education has not kept up with the changing world and children are attending an obsolete educational system. He often says that going to school, getting good grades, and finding a secure job is the most dangerous advice one can give a child.

He believes that today's children can't achieve financial security if they play by the old rules. They need more sophisticated education than what schools currently provide. They have to know the rules. The rich and the 95% of the population play by different rules of money. The 95% acquires the rules in school and at home. He believes that an archaic school system can't teach subjects it doesn't know.

Sharon agreed to co-author Robert's book that will help people educate themselves and their children about money and other financial matters.

At a young age, Kiyosaki was already aware of his desire to be wealthy. He was lucky that he had a "rich" father figure who was willing to teach him. He believes that education lays the groundwork for success, but financial and communications skills are equally as vital.

This book is about the story of Kiyosaki's two dads and the skills he has developed. Sharon Lecther says that she has supported, edited, and assembled the book. While many of the theories may challenge core accounting principles, they offer an invaluable insight into the analytical processes that goes into every investment decisions made by actual investors.

By the age of 16, Robert knew that he wanted to own corporation. He was enthusiastic to begin growing his assets but he realized that a college education is beneficial.

Sharon admits that the ideas in the book may be too radical and incredible for today's parents. She says, however, that parents have to open their mind to innovative and daring ideas. She cites the need for new approaches to education and suggests that it is not a bad idea for parents to advise their children to be ideal employees while working towards acquiring their own corporation.

Sharon Lechter ends the chapter by challenging her fellow parents to either play safe or play smart by educating themselves and developing their children's financial talent.

# Chapter 1: Rich Dad, Poor Dad

Robert Kiyosaki begins by telling his readers that he had two fathers. He described one as rich and the other one as poor. The two fathers were poles apart in their educational achievements and their approach to life and money. While both fathers worked hard and did well in their respective careers, their lives ended differently. One dad left a legacy of riches to his family and beneficiaries, while the other bequeathed debts. While the two dads believed in education, they offered contrasting advice on the course of study that he should pursue.

Even at such a young age, Kiyosaki found himself in a rare position of having to compare and choose between two different points of view. It was a challenging situation because at the time, they were both beginning their career and are struggling financially.

The two dads also had conflicting views about money. One believes that evil stems from the love of money while the other believes that evil is caused by the lack of money. Both dads have strong personalities. The odd situation pushed him to analyze things independently, a choice which would benefit him in the long run.

Kiyosaki believes that rich people get richer and poor people get poorer because they learn about the concept of money at home from their parents. The poor parents pass on the same money principles they have lived by to their children. A poor parent will typically just advise their child to work hard at school. They may excel in their education but end up with the mindset and financial programming of a poor person.

Schools train students to acquire professional skills but don't teach them about financial skills. Kiyosaki cited this as the reason why academically successful people are struggling financially. He attributed the country's staggering debt levels to highly educated leaders and decision makers who have limited training about money.

He expressed apprehension for the future and the possibility of having millions of people who will be entirely dependent on the government for financial and medical support. He fears about the country's survival if children's financial education remains on the hands of their own parents.

Kiyosaki learned about money from his two fathers. However, he pondered further about each father's advice and this helped him gain valuable insight into the effect and power of thoughts on a person's life. While the poor dad would typically say he can't afford something, the rich dad would ask how he can afford it. He learned from the rich dad that the brain cease to work when one says he can't afford it. On the other hand, asking how one can afford it activates the brain.

The rich dad preached about exercising the mind. He believed that his brain was getting stronger each day because he was exercising it and that the stronger it becomes, the more he becomes capable of making money. Kiyosaki thought that his poor dad was the opposite. Ultimately, one dad achieved financial success while the other slipped into failure. He realized that the proper use of brain increases one's opportunities to achieve wealth while laziness can cause wealth to decline.

Kiyosaki cites the contrasting attitudes of his two dads. The poor dad believed that the rich should pay more taxes to provide for the poor. The rich dad believed that taxes penalizes productive people and favors non-productive ones.

Both dads advised him to study hard, but for different reasons. For one dad, studying hard will help him land a job at a good company. For the other dad, studying hard will equip him with the skills to find and acquire a good company. One attributes his lack of wealth to the fact that he has children, while the other cites his children as the reason why he is rich.

While one dad encouraged discussions on business and money at the dinner table, the other dad was averse to such talks over meals. One dad cautioned against taking financial risks. The other advised him to learn how to manage risks. One dad considered their home as their family's biggest investment and top asset while the other considered it a liability. While both dads religiously paid their bills, one dad paid his bills first while the other settled his bills last.

One dad trusted that the government or employer will provide for the needs of their constituents or workers. He was focused on salary increases and other work benefits. His idea of success was enjoying lifetime entitlement package after retirement. He gave more importance to tenure, job security, and compensation than the job itself. Having worked hard for the government, he felt entitled to these benefits.

The other dad advocated self-reliance and financial competence. He blamed the entitlement mentality for producing financially-dependent people. One dad found it difficult to save cash while the other dad invested. One dad taught him to prepare an impressive resume to help him land a good job while the other taught him how to prepare strong financial and business plans, which could help him create jobs.

Kiyosaki considers himself fortunate to have two strong dads because it allowed him to observe how different thoughts could impact a person's life. He observed that people's life is shaped by their thoughts. He cited his poor dad who always said that he'll never be rich and how this has become a reality. Quite the opposite, the other dad always called himself rich and did things the way rich people do them.

The poor dad always downplayed money and its importance. The rich dad extolled money and equates it to power. At a young age, Kiyosaki learned to be aware of his thoughts and expressions and the need to discern which thoughts he would imbibe as his own.

Kiyosaki had to decide who to listen to between his two dads. One dad wanted him to take the traditional route of earning a degree and getting a good job to earn money. That dad encouraged him to become an accountant, a lawyer, or a professional or to earn an MBA. While the other dad also encouraged him to get a strong education, his focus was on studying to be rich, mastering money, and making it work for him. The rich dad repeatedly said that he doesn't work for money and that money works for him.

Kiyosaki chose to take the rich dad's advice about money. His decision to turn away from his highly educated but poor dad's financial advice and attitude on money was a painful one but it was this decision that would shape his life. His financial education started at the age of 9 after he made that decision. The rich dad mentored him for 30 years.

Kiyosaki argues that financial education is more powerful than money. Financial education equips a person with skills to gain control of money and to start creating wealth. People are working hard for money instead of mastering money because they didn't learn how money works.

Kiyosaki shares the six major lessons he learned from his rich dad in this book.

# Chapter 2: Lesson One: The Rich Don't Work For Money

When he was nine, Kiyosaki approached his dad to ask him how he could get rich. Earlier in the day, Jimmy, one of classmates, bluntly told him that he and Mike were not invited to their beach house for the weekend because they were poor kids.

The year was 1956. Robert was attending a public school where the affluent and influential people in the sugar plantation town sent their kids from grades one to six. Their children were later sent to private schools after completing the sixth grade. Robert and Mike were enrolled at this school only because they lived on that side of the street.

His dad told him that he has to learn to make money if he wants to be rich. When he asked him how he'll make money, his father told him to use his head. Robert assumed that his father didn't know the answer.

The following day, a Saturday, he related the conversation

he had with his father to Mike, his best friend. They weren't categorically poor but they felt like that because the rest of their classmates always flashed the trending stuff or gadgets. On the other hand, Robert's parents only provided the basic needs. His dad had always advised him to work for something he wanted.

The two boys agreed to be partners in their mission to make money. They spent the entire morning brainstorming on ideas to make money. The thought of their classmates having fun at the beach house hurt them both but it also inspired them to use their heads to come up with ideas to make money. They finally stumbled on an idea that Mike had read in his science book. A partnership was sealed at that moment.

The next few weeks saw the partners making the rounds of their neighbors and asking them to save their toothpaste tubes for them. They stockpiled the tubes in a brown cardboard box and placed it beside his mom's washing machine. The sight of the mess had gotten to her mom who threatened to throw the materials if they didn't do something about them. They were given a one-week deadline with a threat of eviction. The partners had no choice but to move their production to an earlier date.

One day, his dad drove up with his friend and saw the two boys working in the driveway where they had set the production line. The area was noticeably littered with fine white powder. The boys had placed several milk cartons and a grill on a long table. The hibachi grill glowed with red hot coals.

His father and friend approached them, and saw the toothpaste tubes being melted down on a steel pot. When asked what they were doing, the boys replied that they were making money. His father realized that they were casting nickels and *literally* making money. The boys were shocked to learn that they were actually making counterfeit money.

Robert's father complimented the boys for their creativity and originality, and even encouraged them to continue. Robert asked his dad why he wasn't rich. His dad replied that he wasn't rich because he had opted to be a school teacher and being rich is not something that people like him think about.

He told him that he lacked the knowledge to make money

and could not help them. He advised them to ask Mike's dad about the subject. He related that their banker was impressed with his brilliance in money making. Mike was incredulous and asked why they didn't have a nice house and car. Robert's father explained that possessing a nice house and car didn't mean that a person is rich or knows how to make money.

Robert's father said that he was no different from Jimmy's dad who is an employee at a sugar plantation. Jimmy's dad is using a company car. He may end up unemployed because the company is going through some rough times. Mike's dad is different because he was building a business empire and will likely become rich in a few years.

Mike arranged a meeting with his dad who agreed to see them on Saturday morning.

The two boys met Mike's dad at 8 o'clock in the morning. Robert observed that Mike's home was small, simple, and tidy. It was a noticeably aging house with creaking wooden floors. He noted a cheap mat near the door that was clean but obviously worn out and needed replacement. He entered the narrow living room with Mike and found two women sitting on the couch and a man in polished work clothes sitting across them. Mike told him that they work for his dad. The boys headed out to the porch where Mike's dad had agreed to meet them.

Mike's dad made them an offer. He agreed to teach them how to make money. He asked them to work for him first. Robert wanted to ask a question but Mike's father dismissed him. He told them that the ability to know when to make quick decisions is a valuable skill as opportunities come and go. He gave the boys ten seconds to decide to either take it or leave it. The boys agreed to take the offer.

The boys were told that they can ride with Mrs. Martin later that morning and start working. They were asked to work for three hours every Saturday for which they will be paid 10 cents per hour. Robert opted to take the offer although it meant he would be missing his softball game.

Robert and Mike worked for Mrs. Martin on one of the nine superettes owned by Mike dad. These superettes were the predecessors of convenience stores like the 7-11 we are more familiar with today. They were located on large parking lots and sold items like bread, milk, cigarettes, and butter. At the time, air-conditioning was unheard of in Hawaii. The store had two doors – one faced the road while the other faced the parking lot. The doors were left open because of the heat and this caused dust to accumulate inside the store.

The boys started working at about nine in the morning. Mrs. Martin was skillful at delegating tasks and kept the boys working. Robert and Mike spent the next three hours removing the dust from each canned goods on the shelves. They had to remove each can and rearrange them neatly after dusting them off with a feather duster. The job was both exhausting and tiresome and the pay was excruciatingly low. Robert spent the money he earned on comic books, which cost a dime each.

On the fourth week, Robert told Mike that he was quitting. Robert ranted about the miserable school lunch, the boring school, and the fact that the job had been preventing him from enjoying his Saturdays. He complained about the measly 30 cents they were getting for the job. Mike told him that his dad was expecting him to quit and would talk to him the next Saturday.

Robert was prepared for the meeting. His real dad expressed his indignation over what he thought was a violation of child labor laws. He though that the matter deserved to be investigated. He advised him to demand the pay that he deserved which should not be lower than 25 cent per hour. He told him to quit immediately if he did not get a raise.

By eight o'clock that Saturday, he was at Mike's house. Mike's dad told him to take a seat and wait for his turn as he went inside his office. He saw the two women who sat on the same couch that first Saturday. The women, as well as an older gentleman, met with Mike's dad. Robert waited for an hour before he was allowed inside the office.

Mike's dad initiated the conversation by telling Robert that he had heard about his plans to quit if not given a raise. Robert almost tearfully confronted the old man for reneging on their agreement to teach him in exchange for his hard work. He accused him of being a crook. He told Mike's dad that he was greedy and unsympathetic towards his employees. He cited the lack of respect he had shown towards him by making him wait.

The older man calmly listened to him, and told Robert that he sounded like most of his employees. Robert went on with his whining and accused the rich dad of not only failing to fulfill his end of the bargain but also of wanting to torment him. He called the act cruel. He accused him of lying. He reminded him of the child labor laws and warned him that his dad was a government employee.

Mike's dad, Robert's Rich dad, told him that he sounded like the people he either fired or had quit the posts they were given. Robert challenged him and asked what he had to say. He continued to accuse him of lying and not teaching him anything in those three weeks that he worked for him.

Rich dad asked Robert if he thought that teaching meant talking or giving a lecture to which the boy replied in the affirmative. Rich dad told him that life is the best teacher yet it doesn't talk to people most of the time. Instead, it just pushes them around which is its way of telling them it wants them to learn something. He told him that he will do well if he learns these lessons from life. If not, he will spend his lifetime putting the blame on his boss, low salary, or job and will just be waiting for breaks.

The rich dad told him that he could also be someone who will choose to play safe and do the right things while waiting for something that never comes. That type of person wants to win but is too scared to take risks.

Robert realized that the rich dad was allowing him and Mike to have a taste of life. The rich dad's lesson started to sink in. When he asked what the solution should be, the rich dad gently tapped his dead to tell him that the answer is in his mind.

In this chapter, Kiyosaki shares what he frequently heard from his rich dad about the big disparity in money principles between the rich and the middle class or poor people. While the middle class and poor people work for money, wealthy people make money work for them.

At a young age, Kiyosaki was able to see the disparity between his two dads' attitude towards money. The rich dad didn't believe in having more money as the solution. He wanted him to learn how to control money and make it work for him.

The rich dad had them work without pay for the next three weeks. This challenged the boys to seek an alternative way to earn money. Robert saw an opportunity to make money with old comic books. He and Mike offered them for a small fee to other kids.

# Chapter 3: Lesson Two: Why Teach Financial Literacy

Robert Kiyosaki and Mike's story continues in Chapter 3. In 1990, both were already adults who have achieved tremendous success in their financial and social status.

Mike took his dad's lessons seriously and applied them to his life. He inherited his dad's business empire and had been effectively managing its affairs. He was training his son as his successor in the same way that his dad trained him and Kiyosaki.

While Mike had opted to manage the business empire, Kiyosaki and his wife had chosen to retire in 1994. He was 47 while his wife was 37. By then, working is optional and their wealth is substantial enough to grow on its own. Kiyosaki likened it to planting a tree that one nourishes for years until it has grown enough to subsist on its own. It then gives shade and becomes a source of pleasure for its owner.

In his speaking engagements, people frequently asked

Kiyosaki for the secrets to his success. They sought his advice on how to train their children and how to start. Kiyosaki shares an article he once read.

The article tells of a meeting among the most affluent businessmen and greatest leaders held at Edgewater Beach Hotel in 1923. The group consisted of Samuel Insull, Leon Frazier, Ivar Kreuger, Charles Schwab, Albert Fall, Arthur Cotton, Jesse Livermore, Richard Whitney, and Howard Hopson. The group discussed various money schemes and investment issues. After twenty-five years, those who attended the meeting either ended up or died penniless, broke, insane, or in jail. The main lesson that can be derived from the tragic endings of such great men is that financial literacy is a must to sustain the wealth and keep it safe.

The debacle that hit the best entrepreneurs in the 1920's can still be seen at present times in the professional sports when top-earning athletes make unwise financial decisions and end up with nothing. Kiyosaki noted that 1997 produced many instant millionaires. He cautioned that, ultimately, what matters is how much one keeps and how many generations keep it.

The lesson intends to teach people to learn how to manage or control money before they have it. It teaches people to build a strong foundation first before they embark on achieving their dreams. His rich dad emphasized the importance of financial literacy as complementary to one's drive to become rich. Anyone aspiring to be rich should learn the basics of accounting.

Mike and Kiyosaki were fortunate for having a rich dad who taught them to lay down a solid foundation. Rich dad initially used drawn pictures and words to teach the two boys the language and flow of money. As they grew older, he gradually added numbers.

Kiyosaki shares that there's only one rule to remember and that is to know how to *differentiate between assets and liabilities* and to acquire assets. This was the rich dad's answer to the boys' question on how they can be rich, the secret they have waited for years to hear.

Rich dad repeatedly said that a person who wants to get rich has to read and comprehend numbers. Rich people accumulate assets while middle class and poor people accumulate liabilities.

Kiyosaki shared basic diagrams illustrating the relationships between income, expenses, assets, and liabilities. He provided simple working definition of asset and liability. He defined an asset as anything that adds cash to one's purse while he described a liability as anything that reduces the money in one's purse. He described how the flow of cash differs between the rich and the poor or middle or class. Financially successful people buy assets throughout their lifetime. On the other, the middle class and poor people buy expenses and grow their liabilities.

# Chapter 4: Lesson Three: Mind Your Own Business

In Chapter 4, Kiyosaki uses McDonald's to introduce the readers to the concept of real estate investing. People often assume that McDonald's business is selling hamburgers but its owner and founder, Ray Kroc, tells them that his business is real estate. McDonald's owns the prime land where its branches are located.

Kiyosaki advises those who want to get rich to **start their own** business instead of working for their employer's business. He encourages his readers to become self-sufficient by becoming their own boss and growing their own company.

He continues to discuss asset building, teaching his readers that real assets are those that have value and they include income-generating real estate, mutual funds, bonds, stocks, royalties, and notes. He shares his preferences for investment which are stocks and real estate. He reveals that he started small in real estate investing and would later trade his properties for larger properties. He delays the payment of taxes for capital gains by taking advantage of an IRS mechanism.

# Chapter 5: Lesson Four: The History of Taxes and the Power of the Corporation

Kiyosaki cites the difference between the poor and the rich when it comes to their attitude to big corporations. The poor allow the big corporations to manipulate them while the rich know how to handle them. The rich possess the knowledge and confidence to harness the corporation's powers and turn them to their advantage.

The author describes the tax advantages that corporation enjoy over individual taxpayers. While individuals are taxed on their earnings and have to subsist on what's left after the taxes, corporations are taxed on what's left of its earnings after spending whatever it can. Kiyosaki says that individuals are possibly not aware of the extent by which they are being manipulated. They work hard to remit taxes off their income to the government while the rich are using their knowledge to legally avoid being taxed.

Kiyosaki advises his readers to develop their financial IQ in order to rise out of their situations. They can achieve this by empowering themselves with the knowledge of the law, investing, accounting, and the stock market. He cautions that ignorance is the reason why people are being manipulated and that being informed gives them the power to overcome barriers to being rich.

# Chapter 6: Lesson Five: The Rich Invent Money

Kiyosaki starts the chapter by sharing the story of Alexander Graham Bell. The young man had just patented his invention, the telephone, and demand was overwhelming that he was having problems coping. His small company was simply not prepared for it so he approached Western Union and tried to sell his patent and company for $100,000. The big company balked at the amount and rejected his proposal. The rejection resulted in the emergence of a multi-billion-dollar industry and AT&T.

The author tells of a news story about a massive lay off undertaken by a local company. The retrenched workers accused the management of not being fair while a manager who had been terminated was pleading for the guards to allow him to speak to the owners. He has a wife and two children, and was afraid that he might lose the house he had just purchased recently.

The author tells his readers that everyone has enormous potential and talent but is *held back by self-doubt and the lack of self-confidence.* Most will realize that the real world is more than just having degrees and excellent grades. Kiyosaki says people variably call that factor <u>guts, audacity, brilliance, chutzpah, daring, bravado, or cunning</u>. It's this factor that ultimately decides how one fares in life.

Kiyosaki says that each person has a daring, brave, and brilliant character that has a reverse side which is ready to grovel when the situation demands. He says that extreme fear and doubts are the enemies of one's genius. The person with guts often outpaces the smart person. One needs to be both technically knowledgeable and courageous. Kiyosaki shares that he encourages his students to take risks and allow their talent to turn their fears to excellence and power.

The author tells his readers to take risks and enhance their financial know-how in order to have more options in life. He foresees that there will be more people like Bell and Bill Gates as well as successful companies like Microsoft. On the other hand, business failures and retrenchment will also be common occurrences.

Kiyosaki shares that he is developing his financial know

how because he prefers to welcome change than dread it and that he would choose getting enthusiastic about amassing wealth than brooding about salary increases.

He describes the information age as an exciting era where people with highly developed financial IQ can prosper. On the other hand, it will be a terrifying time for people who play safe and hold on to their to age old concepts. The information age will produce large batches of megamillionaires as well as leave many people behind.

The author expressed his observation that resistance to change has caused people to struggle. These are the same people who blame everything but themselves for their misfortunes. They are saddled with well-worn ideas that have become their major liability.

Kiyosaki introduces a game he had created called CASHFLOW. He shares that since 1984, he has been using simulation and games to teach people about money management and investing.

# Chapter 7: Lesson Six: Work to Learn - Don't Work for Money

In this chapter, Kiyosaki discusses the important skills that individuals should develop to achieve financial success.

He cites a young lady reporter who held a Master's Degree in English Literature as an example. Kiyosaki was impressed with the lady reporter's writing style, but she herself recognized that her writing career was not advancing. Kiyosaki advised her to take a sales course but she was offended by the suggestion. She felt that she had worked hard for her degree and that it would be demeaning for her to learn how to sell.

Kiyosaki shares the case of a brilliant young mechanic who was able to fix his car in a few minutes. He was amazed at the way the young man was able to diagnose what's wrong with the car by simply listening to its engine.

The author uses the examples of the young news reporter and the mechanic to emphasize that it's not enough to have great talent. People need to learn other important skills to help them achieve financial freedom. There are many highly educated and gifted people who don't do well in life. Many lack just one skill to achieve enormous wealth.

The author describes financial intelligence as a combination of knowledge in investing, accounting, law, and marketing. He also cites the need to develop communication skills.

# Chapter 8: Overcoming Obstacles

The author believes that there are five personality traits that can hinder a financially literate person march towards financial independence.

### *Fear*

Kiyosaki says that everyone harbors fears of losing money. There is, however, a big difference in how the rich and the poor manage this fear. What's important is how one handles fear, losing money, and failure.

The author contends that the power of compound interest is the reason why there is a big difference between people who start saving early and those who save later in life. Hence, people who start saving young will have an easier time enriching themselves.

Kiyosaki tells the story of a neighbor who has been working for 25 years with a large computer company and was looking forward to retirement in five years time. His 401k retirement plan was heavily invested in large-growth mutual funds and he expects to leave his job with $4 million in the plan. He plans to convert the mutual funds to government securities and bonds from which he can look forward to a passive annual cash flow well above the $300,000 mark.

The author thinks that this is an example that shows it is possible to make oneself financially well-off in spite loathing both risk and losing. He emphasizes the importance of starting early, setting up a retirement plan, and hiring a trustworthy financial planner who can dispense valuable investment advice.

While his poor dad evaded the subject of retiring early and taking risks, his rich dad advised him to emulate the attitude of a Texan towards risk, losing, and winning. Texans, according to him, take great pride in victory and brag about their losses. They live it big because if they have to go broke, *they might as well do it big*. He argues that playing it too safe is the biggest reason for not achieving financial success. People fail to achieve their financial goals mostly because they regard the pain of financial loss as more overwhelming than the pleasures of being wealthy.

The rich dad often told Robert and Mike the story of

Alamo whenever he would embark on a big business venture or had to take a risk. The Texans attitude towards failure strengthened his resolve and reminded him that he could always find ways to convert monetary losses to gains.

Kiyosaki tells his readers that winners are not afraid to lose. On the contrary, failures inspire winners. Most people lose money because of their fear of losing money.

While the author believes that keeping a safe and balanced investment portfolio is better than not having any, he advocates being focused over being balanced if one wants to have a winning portfolio. The author mentions well-known personalities like Bill Gates, George Patton, Donald Trump, and Thomas Edison and describes them as focused, not balanced. He believes that people who want to be rich need to focus and invest significantly in a few baskets. He cautions against placing few eggs in numerous baskets like what the middle class and poor people do.

For people who abhor losing and are unable to handle defeat, he encourages them to play safe and settle for balanced investing but advises them to begin building their nest egg early. He further tells people who crumble in the face of defeat to hold on to their day job or invest in relatively safer instruments like bonds or mutual funds.

## Cynicism

The author uses the Chicken Little story to demonstrate that all people have doubts. Doubts and fears can immobilize a person. Some of these doubts are self-doubts while some are raised by the constant reminders of loved ones and friends about one's shortcomings. Cynicism can push a person to inaction. It can cause a person to forego opportunities. A person needs to have courage in order to avoid being swamped by doomsayers. The author claims that doubts can cripple and prevent a person from getting rich.

Kiyosaki tells his readers that the Chicken Little in cynics prevents them from thinking clearly and analyzing. He believes that understanding of the "stop" mechanism in stock investing will encourage more people to invest to win. He explains that the "stop" is a computer instruction that causes the investor's stocks to be sold automatically when prices start dropping. This investing feature can help curtail losses and allow the investor to get the most of gains. People who are afraid of losing will benefit greatly from this tool.

The rich dad advised Kiyosaki to emulate Colonel Sanders. After losing his business at age 66, Colonel Sanders started to live off his Social Security check. Since this was insufficient for his needs, he made the rounds of the country to try to sell his fried chicken recipe. <u>It took more than a thousand rejections</u> before he was able to find someone who was willing to buy the recipe. His courage and tenacity helped make him a multimillionaire just when most people his age are quitting.

### *Laziness*

The author claims that people who are busy are frequently the laziest people. He cites an example of a hardworking businessman who was a good provider for his family. One day, his family left him. The businessman knew that their marriage was in trouble but he had chosen to avoid confronting the issue and focused on his work instead of working on their relationship. He was broken and his work performance dipped. He eventually lost his job. There are many other people like him who prefer to divert themselves from issues they don't want to confront. It is a fairly common manifestation of laziness.

Kiyosaki teaches his readers that the cure for laziness is a little greed. Rich dad wanted his children to ask **how** they can afford something, because saying that *one can't afford it* inhibits the brain from working. He also believes that a person's spirit is extremely powerful that it has the ability to discern a lie from the truth. He felt that it is a lie to say that one can't afford something and the human spirit is aware of it. Uttering this lie is a manifestation of laziness and it leads to an inner battle between the mind and spirit.

On the other hand, finding ways to afford something strengthens one's mind and develops a vigorous spirit. Rich dad was more interested in the way a person achieves the objective and not the goal itself. He wasn't the type who would hand his kids anything on a silver platter. Mike and Robert paid for college on their own.

Most people are commonly conditioned from childhood to feel guilty about greed. A person has to learn to ask what he or she stands to gain by achieving something. The best cure for laziness is just a little greed.

## Bad Habits

When Kiyosaki asked the rich dad about the habits of the rich, he responded through an example. After learning from Robert that his own dad pays the bills on the first day of the month and has very little money left after, Rich dad told him that this habit is causing him to struggle financially.

Rich dad told him that he pays himself first before paying his bills on time. He does the same even though his funds aren't enough. He says that he gives more priority to his asset column over the government. He pays his bills on time but only after paying himself. Once this is done, he knows that he will be under pressure to pay his creditors so he has to find more ways to earn money. *It serves as his motivation to find other sources of income and work harder.*

Paying oneself last will ease that pressure but will leave him broke. Fear of the bill collectors motivated him to start businesses, stock trading, and work on extra jobs.

The rich dad explained that paying himself first makes him

stronger financially while paying himself last makes him weaker. He realized that not having good money have allowed people like tax collectors, landlords, and bosses to manipulate him.

### *Arrogance*

Arrogance is the fifth reason for failure and it is a combination of ego and ignorance. The rich dad taught the author that his knowledge had allowed him to make money while his ignorance had caused him to lose money. He would often tell Kiyosaki that he loses money whenever he is overtaken by his own arrogance. Being arrogant made him believe that anything he didn't know was unimportant.

Kiyosaki tells his readers that not a few people attempt to camouflage their ignorance by being arrogant. He would frequently experience this when talking with accountants and fellow investors about financial reports. The author has the impression that there are many finance professionals who are practically clueless about the subject they are discussing. To cure ignorance in any field, the author advises his readers to educate themselves with the help of an industry expert or by reading a relevant book.

# Chapter 9: Getting Started

Kiyosaki presents ten strategies that can help people develop their natural talents and start building their personal wealth.

## 1. Find a reason greater than reality.

The author advises his readers to find a compelling reason or purpose to succeed. He demonstrates this tip by listing down some personal deep-seated emotional desires and 'don't wants' that has strengthened and helped him overcome challenges and endure hardships on the road to getting rich.

His wants included being free and travelling around the world while he is still young, having control over his life and time, and having money work for him.

On the other hand, he abhors working for life and being an employee. He is not satisfied with his parents' aspiration for job security and living in a suburban house. He lamented that this father was too busy making money that he didn't have time to watch his football games. He didn't like the way the government has taken over most of his father's assets after the old man died.

## 2. Choose daily.

The author says that people have the power to choose to be rich, middle class, or poor. He contends that a person acquires the power of making good choices by feeding the mind,

He made a choice as a young boy to be rich and he learned that he only needed to acquire real assets to achieve this. Although Mike has inherited his asset column, he still needed to make a decision to earn the skills to keep it. The author says that he makes the choice to be rich every day.

Kiyosaki advises his readers to invest in education. He shares how his investment of $385 on a three-day real estate seminar has helped him earn $2 million or more. That single course has allowed him to quit working. The author cautions the readers about being arrogant and critical as these traits can impede an individual's learning progress. Keeping an open mind and being humble enough allows one to tap the thinking prowess of great investors like Peter Lynch, George Soros, Warrant Buffett, or Donald Trump.

### 3. Choose friends carefully.

Kiyosaki seeks friends he can learn from and deliberately learns from them. He learns from rich friends who enjoy talking about money and from those who are struggling financially. He warns his readers against listening to Chicken Littles or people who sow doubts and fears.

### 4. Master a formula and learn a new one.

Making money involves following a formula. Most people adhere to a formula they learned from school, which is working for money. The author calls this the basic formula. A person can easily change the formula for making money if the current formula is not producing enough or has become tiresome.

Kiyosaki shares that he learned a formula from a weekend class on buying real estate foreclosures. He dedicated his spare time during the next three years mastering foreclosure buying. He earned millions by applying the formula. In time, the field had become saturated and slow and he decided to look for other formulas. Kiyosaki constantly sought a quicker formula. He believes that being a fast learner is an invaluable skill.

## 5. Pay yourself first.

The author considers self-discipline as the top difference between the rich, the middle class, and the poor. He contends that the absence of internal fortitude is the reason why people are being manipulated.

He believes that a person should be highly skilled in managing cash flow, people, and personal time before starting a business. These three management skills are applicable to the other aspects of a person's life. Mastering self-discipline enhances these skills.

Kiyosaki cites the book "The Richest Man in Babylon" as the source of the "pay yourself first" concept. It is a powerful statement that is often repeated but rarely practiced. He presents diagrams representing the financial statements of people who pay themselves first and those who don't.

People who pay themselves first apportion their monthly income to their asset column before paying for their expenses. The author shares how he always chooses to apply this principle to his finances. Because of his desire to pay himself first, he doesn't rack up excessive credit card debts and unnecessary debts. He minimizes his income to avoid handing it out to government.

Kiyosaki says that his income is generated by his asset column through a corporation. He argues that if he opts to work for money, it just goes to the government. He pays his bills last but he is financially smart enough to avoid getting into tight money situations. He disavows consumer debts. He admits to incurring liabilities but says that these are being paid for by his tenants.

Hence, the first rule in paying oneself first is to not incur huge debts to begin with. The author stresses the importance of prioritizing asset build up and controlling expenses.

The second rule is to avoid dipping into one's savings or investments when short of money. The author advises his readers to allow the pressure to mount and motivate their inner financial intelligence to find more ways to make money.

## 6. Pay your brokers well.

The author shares that he is emulating his rich dad's

practice of compensating professionals fairly. He believes that their expertise and services enable their clients to make money and that he is only paying a tiny percentage of what he stands to earn. He cites the services of brokers who saves him time and help him make money at the same time. Good brokers provide timely and invaluable information about the market and exert time and effort to educate their clients.

He says, however, that brokers aren't born equal. One has to find a broker who is after the best interests of a client and has the expertise to handle a specific type of investment. He applies the same criteria to his accountant and tax lawyer.

Kiyosaki brings up people management skills and cites middle managers who have failed to move up the ranks. While these managers are well adept in managing people below their rank or their subordinates, they have never learned to work with people who are superior to them in talent, expertise, or position. The author believes that true managerial skill involves managing and fairly compensating people who have the expertise and superior talent in specific fields.

## 7. Be an "Indian Giver".

The author makes a reference to a cultural misunderstanding between the American Indians and first white settlers to underscore the need for an investor to look past the payback period and consider the asset that can be had for free. He tells how the white settlers falsely assumed that the Indians were giving them a blanket as a gift while the Indians only intended to lend it to help them warm themselves. Both sides were upset when the time came for Indians to take it back.

The author contends that adopting an Indian giver strategy is essential to getting rich. A savvy investor is always interested about the rate of return of an investment as well as any freebie he might earn from it. He tells of finding a foreclosed condominium in Arizona for which the bank was asking $60,000. Kiyosaki gave a $50,000 bid. The bank accepted the bid simply because they realized his seriousness when he gave a cashier's check equivalent to his bid amount. His company turned it into a vacation rental and he was able to recoup his investment in three years. His property acquisition makes money for him each month of the year.

The author uses the same strategy with stocks. His broker often calls him to recommend the stock of a company that he thinks is about to rise. Kiyosaki typically moves his funds to this stock and wait up to a month for the value to move up. He would then withdraw his initial investment, which will make the funds available for a new asset. As the fund goes in and out, Kiyosaki acquires an asset for himself at practically no cost. He says that financially intelligent investors need to look beyond ROI and see the asset that they will acquire at no cost at the end of the payback period.

## 8. Use assets to buy luxuries.

A person trying to get rich should have self-discipline and inner fortitude to be able to direct money to earn more money. People who are weak are more likely to extend the expense column. This accounts for their financial hardship and poverty. Kiyosaki cites the tendency of many people to use their credit card to pay for luxuries. He shares that he habitually uses his desire to buy luxuries to motivate himself to invest. Nowadays, most people focus on borrowing money instead of creating money to buy whatever they want.

The author advises his readers to train themselves early to master money. People with low financial intelligence will find themselves overwhelmed by the power of money. They will be working for money for the rest of their life. One has to be smarter than money in order to be its master.

## 9. The need for heroes

Emulating people we idolize or admire is a powerful way to learn. The author shares how he reads about his golf heroes and copies their swings. He also admires people like Peter Lynch, Warren Buffet, Jim Rogers, Donald Trump, and George Soros. He learns a lot by reading about their strategies and he subconsciously acts like them when negotiating deals, analyzing trends, or choosing which stocks to invest in. Having successful people to look up to makes investing look easy.

## 10. Teach and you shall receive.

The tenth step expounds on the power of giving. The

author shares that his rich dad taught him about the necessity of giving. His poor dad gave much through his knowledge and time, but has hardly given money away. On the other hand, his rich dad gave both education and money. He advocated tithing and taught Kiyosaki that if he wants something, he must first give it. His rich dad gave money to charity or church when he was short of funds.

The principle of reciprocity also applies to other aspects like love, friendship, happiness, contacts, and sales. Kiyosaki says that it has always worked for him. When he wants sales, for example, he'll help someone make a sale. In turn, sales come to him. The author believes that the more he teaches, the more he learns.

Kiyosaki argues that there are powers that are smarter that people and it's easier to get to where you want to go if these powers are on your side. For the powers to be generous, one should also be generous.

# Chapter 10: Still Want More? Here are Some to Do's

This chapter provides additional tips to help readers achieve their financial goals. The author provides practical or action tips to supplement the ten steps and philosophies he discussed in the previous chapter.

His first tip is to stop and assess which strategy is working and which isn't working. He advises his readers to stop doing something if it is not viable and to explore other ideas. To find new investing ideas, the author visits bookstores and searches for books with unique and varied subjects. He cites the book written by Joel Moskowitz entitled *"The 16 Percent Solution"*.

Kiyosaki's next tip is to take action. He did exactly what Joel Moskowitz wrote in his book. He says that most people never take action or allow other people to talk them out of a new idea. He advises his readers to find someone who has actual experience on what one wants to do and learn from that person.

The author shares with his readers how the courses he has taken have helped him quit his job and advises them to take new classes.

He cites the merit of making multiple offers for real estate properties. He relates how he had taught a friend to make an offer at half the asking price of the sellers of six properties they were looking into. He rationalizes that the seller actually has no idea of the right price for a property until another offer comes along. Sellers generally overprice their properties. Buyers just have to make offers hoping that a seller might approve it.

Kiyosaki says he makes his offers with an escape clause which he can use in case the seller accepts and he wants out of the deal. He always writes that the deal is subject to his business partner's approval.

He advises the readers to drive, walk, or jog in a specific area for ten minutes once a month. He says that for profit to be realized in deals, the elements of change and bargain must be present. He jogs in a neighborhood he is prospecting for investment. The routine allows him to observe and analyze real estate clues in the area such as signage and moving trucks and gives him the chance to talk to postal carriers, drivers, and retailers. He commends the book *"Beating the Street"* by Peter Lynch because it teaches how to select stocks with growth potentials.

Kiyosaki attributes consumers' poverty to their shopping and investing behavior. Consumers rush to the store and stock up during a sale but run away from stock market crash where stocks are on sale. They shop elsewhere when a store hikes its prices but begin buying when the stocks appreciate its value.

He advises potential investors to look in the proper places. He shares a story where he was able to buy a condominium unit for half the price of the unit beside it. He acquired his unit by shopping at a bank's foreclosure department while the other buyer, a neighbor, sought the services of a broker who has no real property to her name. His neighbor was waiting for the condo unit's price to increase but Kiyosaki told his neighbor that profit is made at the time of purchase, not at the time of sales.

To make profitable deals, Kiyosaki finds people who are eager to purchase and matches them with a seller. He illustrates this by using the story of a friend who wanted to buy land. He found one which was larger and sold a portion to his friend. He kept the rest for himself at no cost. The lesson he wants to impart is to buy big and slice it in pieces. Many end up spending more to acquire less because they think small and limit their search to what they can afford. Anyone can think big.

He tells of calling several friends to ask them to partner with his company in negotiating a favorable deal with dealers to buy computers in bulk quantities. He shares that he has employed the same strategy in stock investing. He blames thinking small, acting alone, and inaction as the reason why people stay small.

Kiyosaki advises readers to learn from the past. He reminds his readers about the success stories of Bill Gates and Colonel Sanders and how all big companies began as small businesses.

The last tip he imparted was to take action. Taking action is necessary before one can achieve financial success.

# Epilogue: How to Pay for a Child's College Education for $7000

In this final chapter, the author shares his final thought and tells a story that demonstrates how financial intelligence can be used to deal with today's common financial problems. He tells how people can pay for their children's education while saving up for retirement.

Kiyosaki uses the story of a friend who once lamented the difficulties of saving up for his children's college education. By then, he had around $12,000 investment in a mutual fund. He calculated that he needed $400,000 to send all four children to college. He only had twelve years to accumulate this fund.

In 1991, Phoenix real estate market was experiencing severe depression. Kiyosaki advised his friend to use part of his mutual fund to purchase a house. His friend's credit was over the limit so it wasn't possible for him to take out a loan from a bank to buy a house. The author encouraged him and assured him that there are other ways to finance the purchase.

They searched for a suitable property and found one in a prime neighborhood. The owner had been retrenched from his company and had to sell the property that day because a job was waiting for him in California. Although he was selling the house for $102,000, Kiyosaki and his friend made an offer for $79,000, which the seller accepted.

The property was under a non-qualifying loan and had a balance of $72,000. This meant that his friend only needed to pay out $7,000 to the seller. Kiyosaki's friend rented the property out as soon as the seller moved. He netted $125 each month on the house after paying the mortgage. He applied the excess $125 to the mortgage to shorten its payment period. They estimated that he would be netting $800 monthly when the first child enters college. There's also an option to sell when the market is favorable.

Three years later, a tenant offered $156,000 for the property. Robert advised him to sell it and take advantage of the benefits of the 1031 Tax-deferred Exchange. The transaction left his friend with almost $80,000. Kiyosaki called another friend in Texas who transferred the tax-deferred funds to a mini warehouse. In three months' time, his friend started to receive income of almost $1,000 monthly. He reinvested the money in mutual funds.

In 1996, he sold the mini storage facility for almost $330,000 and reinvested the proceeds in another property that can generate a monthly income of more than $3,000. His friend knew that his goal of $400,000 was easily attainable. All it took was a combination of common financial intelligence and $7,000.

Kiyosaki's friend will be able to provide for his children's college education and at the same time, start saving for his retirement using the underlying asset. The success of the investment strategy meant that his friend can afford to retire early.

# Conclusion

The book *Rich Dad, Poor Dad* presents empowering insights and inspiring lessons on achieving wealth and financial independence. It is an engaging discussion about mindset and perspectives.

Robert T. Kiyosaki uses the comparison between his rich dad and poor dad to demonstrate how their thoughts about money determined their actions and their outcome. His poor dad represents highly educated and hardworking people who are trapped in the Rat Race and are unable to achieve wealth because they lack financial literacy. His rich dad epitomizes people who use their financial knowledge to grow their wealth.

The following are the key points discussed in the book:

- Financial literacy is a must in today's fast changing world. An individual must learn the fundamentals of investing, accounting, law, and economics to be able to recognize opportunities and take advantage of schemes to protect one's assets and create wealth.

- Don't work for money. Instead, strive to make money work for you by building assets that create money. People who work for money end up being exploited by the company, the government, and the bank.

- Understand the difference between asset and liability. Know what assets are and focus on buying assets instead of increasing expenses and building liabilities.

- Pay yourself first. It takes focus, self-discipline, and internal strength to do it but it has to be done consistently if you want to protect your asset column. Avoid dipping into your savings or investments. Defend your asset fort. Put your inner genius to work and find ways to create more money to settle your liabilities.

- Prioritize your asset column over your company, the government, and the bank. Don't just strive to grow your income. Find ways to grow your assets.

- To get rich, one should strive to buy or own the corporation instead of simply working for one. Employees get taxed on their earnings and can only spend what's left after taxes. Corporations earn and spend liberally and only get taxed on the earnings after the expenses. The rich have the financial and legal skills to take advantage of this loophole.

- Learn about investing before making an investment. Find competent professionals who can guide you in your investing decisions and compensate them fairly for their services. Hire people who are smarter than you and learn from them.

- Find successful people who make investing seem easy and emulate them. Learn to manage risks instead of avoiding them.

- People who start saving and investing in their young age will have an easier time getting rich.

- Take a job for the skills you will learn and not for the money you stand to earn from the job. Take time and invest in courses to improve or acquire new skills.

- If you must spend for luxuries, use your assets to buy them. This means putting your assets to work and using the earnings to spend for the things that you want.

- Don't allow opinions, fears, or cynicism of other people to dictate your actions or lead you to inaction.

- Move on from a failure and always try another approach. This is how you progress and grow from your own mistakes.

# FREE BONUSES

**<u>P.S. Is it okay if we overdeliver?</u>**

Here at Readtrepreneur Publishing, we believe in overdelivering way beyond our reader's expectations. Is it okay if we overdeliver?

Here's the deal, we're going to give you an extremely condensed PDF summary of the book which you've just read and much more...

What's the catch? We need to trust you... You see, we want to overdeliver and in order for us to do that, we've to trust our reader to keep this bonus a secret to themselves? Why? Because we don't want people to be getting our exclusive PDF summaries even without buying our books itself. Unethical, right?

Ok. Are you ready?

Firstly, remember that your book is code: "**READ72**".

Next, visit this link: **http://bit.ly/exclusivepdfs**

Everything else will be self explanatory after you've visited: **<u>http://bit.ly/exclusivepdfs</u>**.

We hope you'll enjoy our free bonuses as much as we enjoyed preparing it for you!

CPSIA information can be obtained
at www.ICGtesting.com
Printed in the USA
BVHW051809020919
557356BV00013B/253/P

9 781690 401964